Process Optimization

A Mathematical Approach

by D. James Benton

software available free online

Preface

In this text we will discuss the mathematical analysis of various processes, which are often used in manufacturing. The objective of this analysis is to optimize one or more aspects of the processes, with the goal of maximizing output (or profit) while minimizing waste (or cost). This type of process optimization supports mathematically based (objective, quantitative) decision-making and ultimately better outcomes. Several approaches are presented through increasingly complex examples. I taught this material for the East Tennessee State University Department of Technology as course ENTC-4247 Industrial Operations Analysis.

All of the examples contained in this book,
(as well as a lot of free programs) are available at...
https://www.dudleybenton.altervista.org/software/index.html

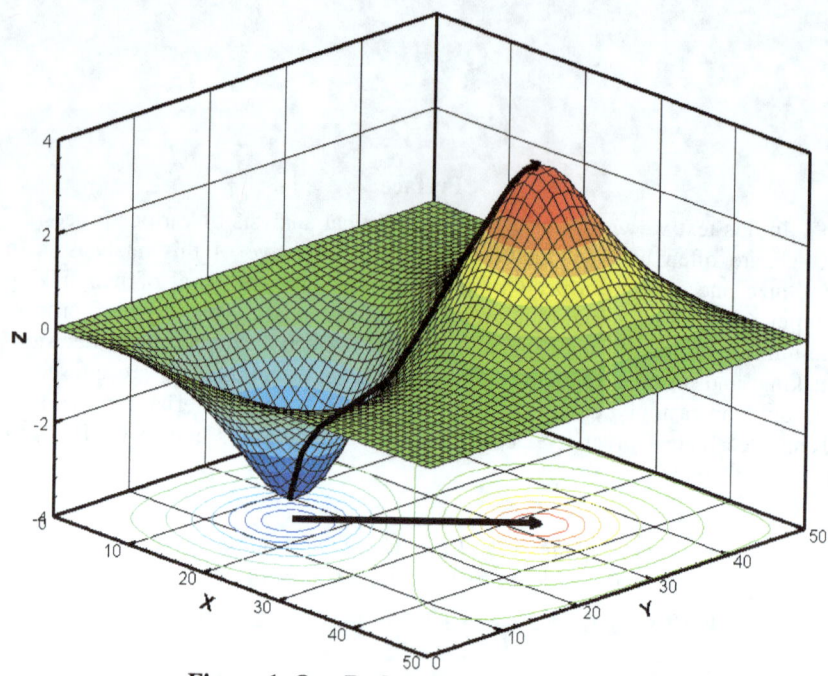

Figure 1. One Path to the Top (maximum)

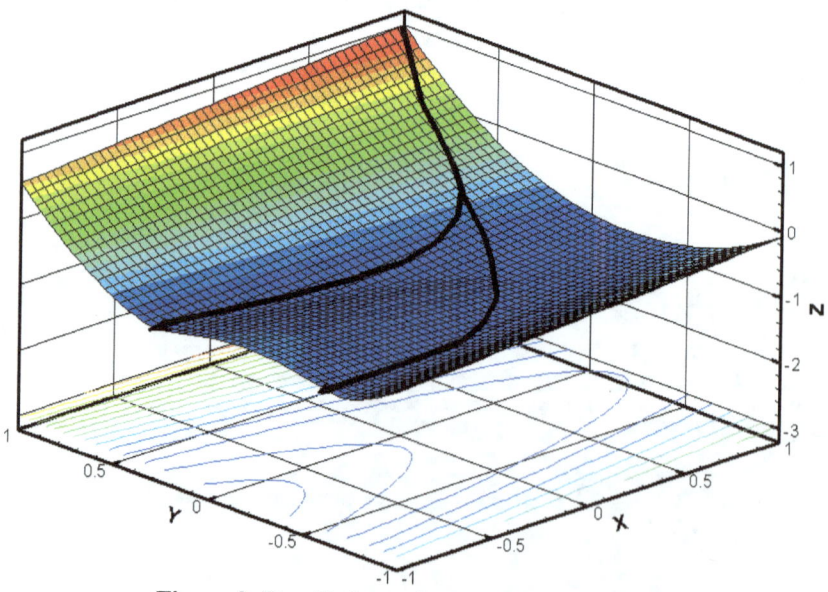

Figure 2. Two Paths to the Bottom (minimum)

Table of Contents

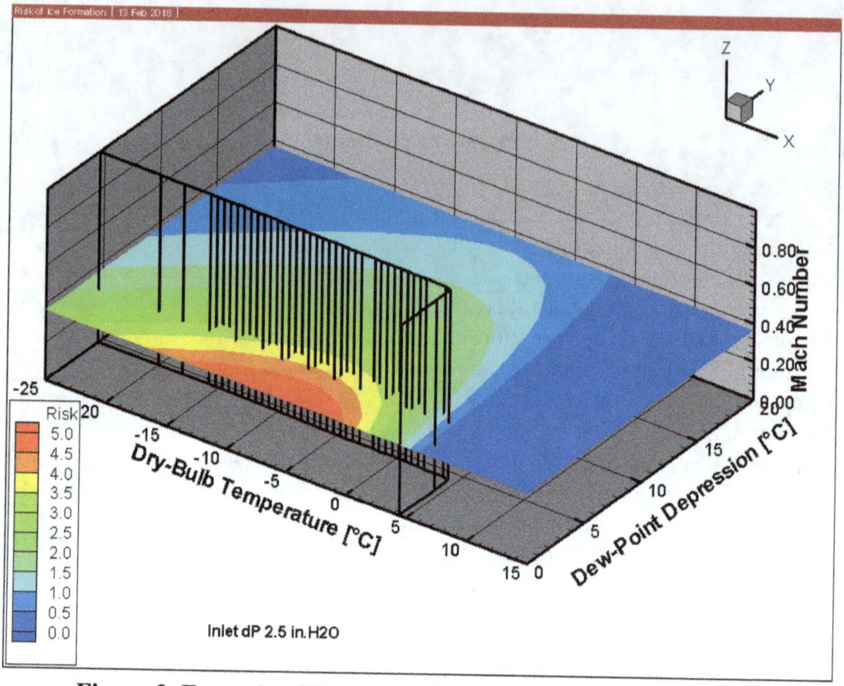

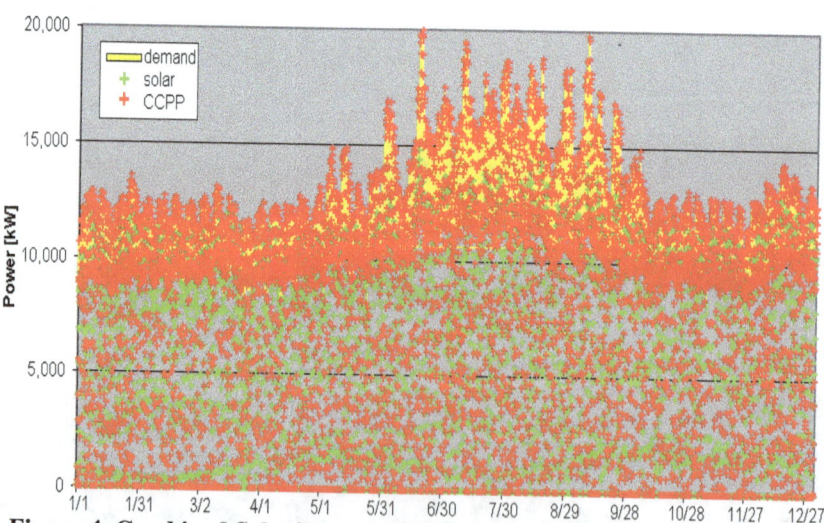

Figure 3. Example of Operational (do not cross this) Boundary

Figure 4. Combined Solar/Gas Turbine Plant Optimized to Meet Demand

Chapter 1. Basic Concepts

Throughout this text we will only consider quantitative measures of productivity, as these can be described and evaluated mathematically. Qualitative measures are important but often do not lend themselves to mathematical analysis or at least the same type of analyses. Concepts such as, "no more than one flaw in a million" are described mathematically as "singular events" which defy calculus.

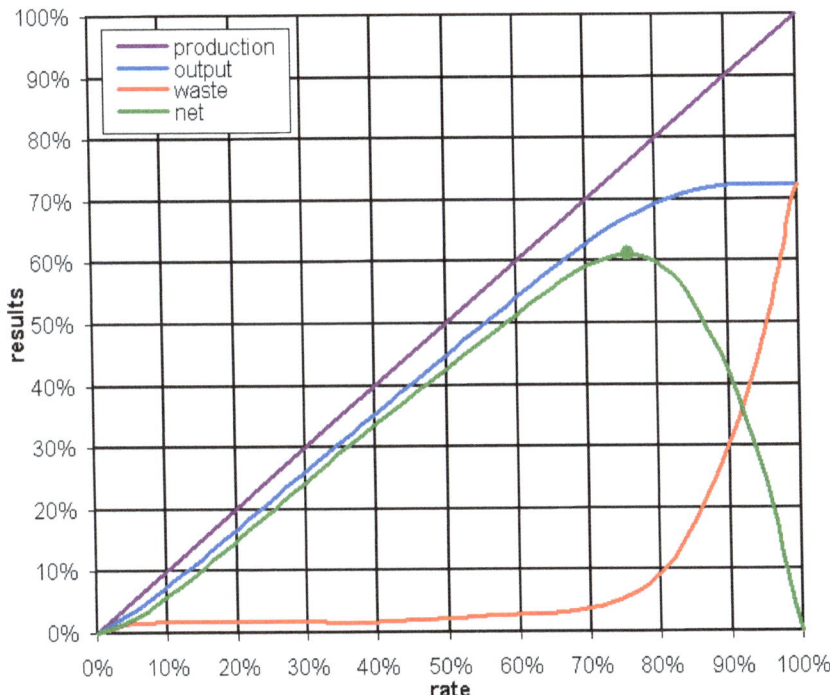

Figure 5. Typical Production Metrics

The production of multiple substantially uniform items (for example: cars, widgets, or pop tarts) involves a process and often many sub-processes. These processes are carried out in a specific location and typically include a team of workers and a collection of equipment. The whole is often referred to as a *line*. This line is operated at some rate, which gives us our first curve. The items are produced at some rate, which gives us a second curve. In every process there is some loss or waste, which may be flaws or other lack of quality, described by a

1

third curve. The total (gross) items minus the loss (or waste) results in the net items produced. Such metrics (i.e., quantitative measures of the process) might look like the figure above.

The purple production line is linear, representing the rate of operation. The blue output curve begins linearly but approaches a constant value (asymptote) of 72.5%. This behavior (curve shape) is common. If this were not the case, one could produce an infinite number of items by simply cranking up the speed. The red waste (or flaw) curve often starts off small, remains fairly constant over a moderate range of operation, but increases sharply at higher rates. "More mistakes happen when you rush any process," is common to many areas of human experience. The green net curve exhibits a peak (maximum net production) of 61% at a rate of 76%. For the process represented by these curves, the optimal operating point is then 76% of the maximum.

Choosing Equipment

Imagine you are given the task of selecting a pump. You have 3 to choose from which are similar in price and durability. The efficiency curves for these pumps are shown in the figure below.

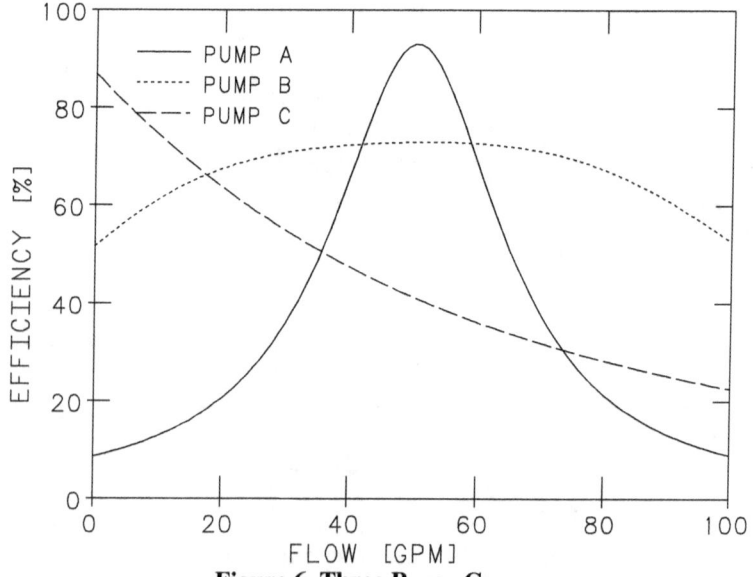

Figure 6. Three Pump Curves

If the pump is expected to operate at a steady rate of 50 gpm (gallons per minute), which one would you choose and why? Pump A is the best choice in this case because it has the highest efficiency at the desired operating point. If the pump is expected to operate over a range of flows from 25 to 75 gpm, which one would you choose and why? In this case Pump B is the best choice because it has the highest efficiency over the expected range of operation. While Pump A

2

would work in this case, the efficiency falls off (becomes less) at lower and higher flows, making it a less-attractive option. The efficiency curve for Pump C is quite unusual. You would only see such in a specialized application. Not only is it desirable to know which device to use, it is also useful to recognize that some designs are targeted and you might use this information later.

Choosing a Schedule

Some operations are considering a 4x10 work week rather than a 5x8. Perhaps the simplest example of this would be one or more assembly lines making widgets. Starting and stopping a process takes time. Reaching peak capacity also takes time. For the purposes of this illustration, we consider such a process under these two staffing scenarios:

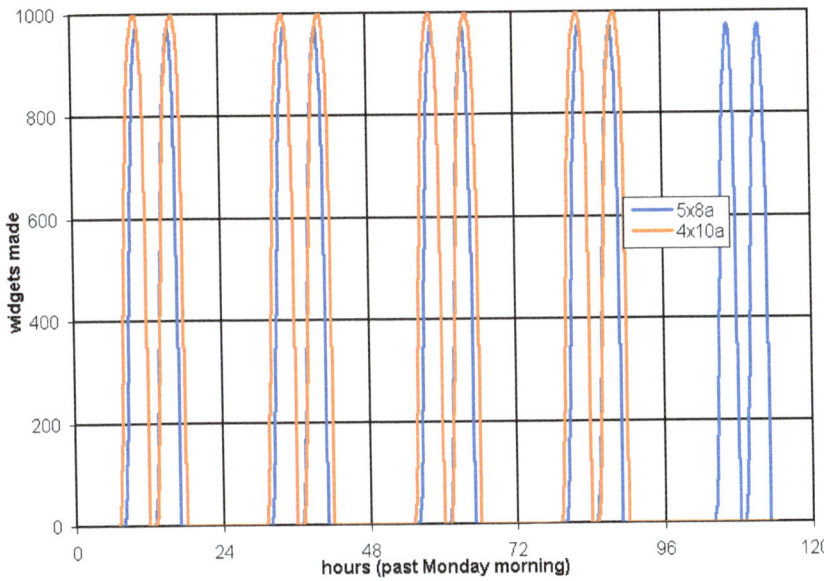

Figure 7. Making Widgets 4x10 or 5x8

The numbers and graphics can be found on the 8or10 tab in spreadsheet simple.xls in the online archive. In this simple example it takes about three and one-half hours to reach peak capacity (1000 widgets every six minutes) plus about an hour and a half to shut down the operation. We first consider a twice per day run with a shutdown mid-day for lunch.

3

This next figure shows a closer look at a single operational period under the two duration scenarios:

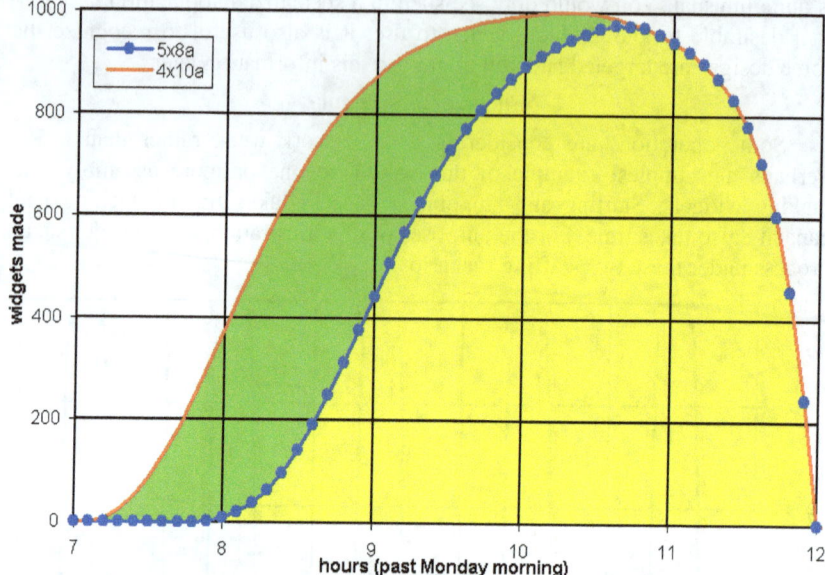

Figure 8. Single Production Cycle Under Two Scenarios

Here we see that the 5x8 schedule never quite reaches the peak of 1000 widgets. For production, we consider the total widgets made, which can be represented by the area under the curve. We see that the 4x10 schedule (orange curve) includes the additional green area, while the 5x8 schedule (blue curve) only includes the yellow. The total widgets made per week is 250,965 for 5x8 or 272,338 for 4x10, which is an increase of 8.5% for the latter, which might seem significant but...

4

We could consider an alternative approach... If the production line requires a full staff to start and stop but only part of the staff to continue at full rate, the mid-day shut down could be eliminated by staggering the lunch break so that the line could continue throughout the day, as shown in this next figure:

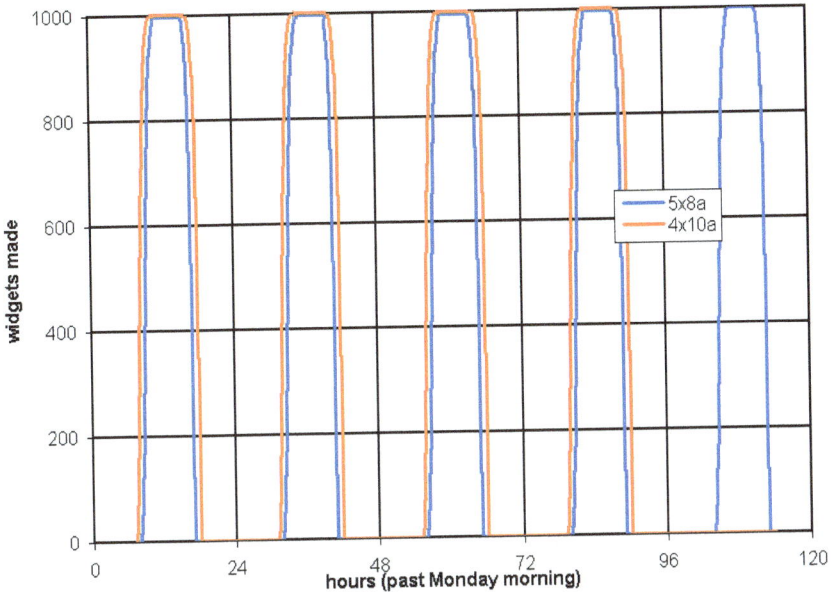

Figure 9. Staggered Lunch Break/Continuous Operation

This would reshape the operational period, as shown in the figure below:

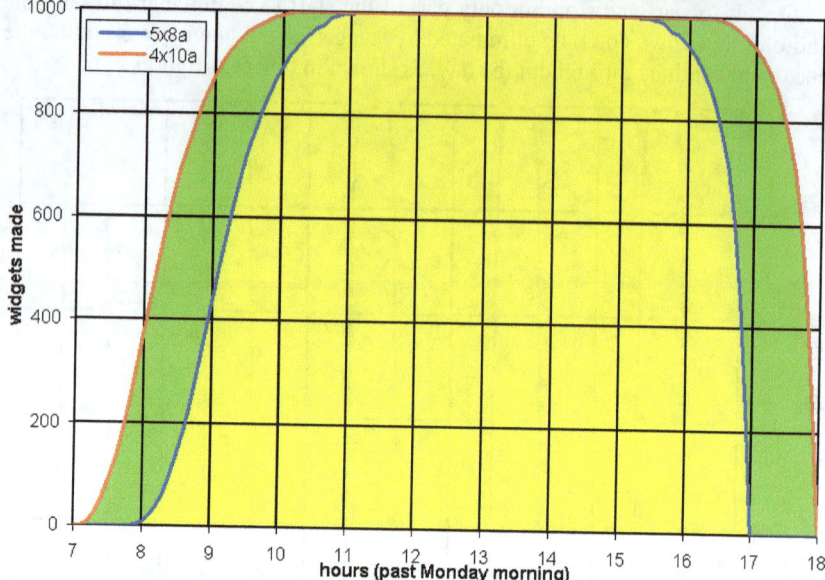

which increases the output for both scenarios to 375,254 and 376,169, respectively for a difference of 0.2%. This illustrates how it can be helpful to express options mathematically and evaluate them before making decisions.

Introduction

This is then the simplest example of Process Optimization: answering the question, "At what rate of operation is the maximum net output achieved?" Actual systems are often more complicated, involve more than one variable, and may also have multiple constraints, such as: You must stop and clean the pop tart assembly line every 12 hours. Such systems require more elaborate mathematics.

I taught this class (ENTC-4247) at a remote campus a few miles from my home. Halfway between the two (home and campus) sits a Tom's™ factory, which made cheese crackers and also peanut butter crackers on the same assembly line. One of the students in that class worked at the Tom's™ factory and described the careful cleaning process followed to assure a food-safe end product. Sadly, the factory has been closed and so is the nearby factory that made vinyl siding.

Chapter 2. Simple Algebraic Examples

Real-world process optimization problems most often present themselves as *word problems*; that is, a series of verbal descriptions of relationships, limitations, and measures. In order to solve these problems, we must transform them into their native algebraic form. Before delving into this transformation, we first consider pure algebraic examples. The first of these being to maximize the value of z, which depends on two variables: x_1 and x_2.

$$z = 3x_1 + 2x_2 \qquad (2.1)$$

This problem is constrained by the following two conditions:

$$2x_1 + x_2 \leq 6$$
$$x_1 + 2x_2 \leq 6 \qquad (2.2)$$

The first constraint looks like this, where the green (T) cells satisfy the constraint and the yellow (F) cells don't...

x1/2	0	1	2	3	4	5	6	7
0	T	T	T	T	T	T	T	F
1	T	T	T	T	T	F	F	F
2	T	T	T	F	F	F	F	F
3	T	F	F	F	F	F	F	F
4	F	F	F	F	F	F	F	F
5	F	F	F	F	F	F	F	F
6	F	F	F	F	F	F	F	F
7	F	F	F	F	F	F	F	F

The second constraint looks like this...

x1/2	0	1	2	3	4	5	6	7
0	T	T	T	T	F	F	F	F
1	T	T	T	F	F	F	F	F
2	T	T	T	F	F	F	F	F
3	T	T	F	F	F	F	F	F
4	T	T	F	F	F	F	F	F
5	T	F	F	F	F	F	F	F
6	T	F	F	F	F	F	F	F
7	F	F	F	F	F	F	F	F

Combining the two constraints and replacing T/F with the z value is shown in this next figure...

x1/2	0	1	2	3	4	5	6	7
0	0	2	4	6	8	10	12	14
1	3	5	7	9	11	13	15	17
2	6	8	**10**	12	14	16	18	20
3	9	11	13	15	17	19	21	23
4	12	14	16	18	20	22	24	26
5	15	17	19	21	23	25	27	29
6	18	20	22	24	26	28	30	32
7	21	23	25	27	29	31	33	35

We then see that the optimum result (z=10), which occurs when $x_1=x_2=2$.

The next example will maximize:

$$z = 2x_1 + 3x_2 \qquad (2.3)$$

subject to four constraints:

$$-3x_1 + x_2 \leq 1$$
$$4x_1 + 2x_2 \leq 20$$
$$4x_1 - x_2 \leq 20 \qquad (2.4)$$
$$-x_1 + 2x_2 \leq 5$$

The first two constraints look like this...

x1/2	0	1	2	3	4	5	6	7
0	T	T	F	F	F	F	F	F
1	T	T	T	T	F	F	F	F
2	T	T	T	T	T	T	T	T
3	T	T	T	T	T	T	T	T
4	T	T	T	T	T	T	T	T
5	T	T	T	T	T	T	T	T
6	T	T	T	T	T	T	T	T
7	T	T	T	T	T	T	T	T

x1/2	0	1	2	3	4	5	6	7
0	T	T	T	T	T	T	T	T
1	T	T	T	T	T	T	T	T
2	T	T	T	T	T	T	T	F
3	T	T	T	T	T	F	F	F
4	T	T	T	F	F	F	F	F
5	T	F	F	F	F	F	F	F
6	F	F	F	F	F	F	F	F
7	F	F	F	F	F	F	F	F

The second two constraints look like this...

x1/2	0	1	2	3	4	5	6	7
0	T	T	T	T	T	T	T	T
1	T	T	T	T	T	T	T	T
2	T	T	T	T	T	T	T	T
3	T	T	T	T	T	T	T	T
4	T	T	T	T	T	T	T	T
5	T	T	T	T	T	T	T	T
6	F	F	F	F	T	T	T	T
7	F	F	F	F	F	F	F	F

x1/2	0	1	2	3	4	5	6	7
0	T	T	T	F	F	F	F	F
1	T	T	T	T	F	F	F	F
2	T	T	T	T	F	F	F	F
3	T	T	T	T	T	F	F	F
4	T	T	T	T	T	F	F	F
5	T	T	T	T	T	T	F	F
6	T	T	T	T	T	T	F	F
7	T	T	T	T	T	T	T	F

8

The combined constraints and z values are shown in this next figure:

x1/2	0	1	2	3	4	5	6	7
0	0	3	6	9	12	15	18	21
1	2	5	8	11	14	17	20	23
2	4	7	10	13	16	19	22	25
3	6	9	12	15	**18**	21	24	27
4	8	11	14	17	20	23	26	29
5	10	13	16	19	22	25	28	31
6	12	15	18	21	24	27	30	33
7	14	17	20	23	26	29	32	35

The solution (optimum result) is z=18, which occurs at $x_1=3$, $x_2=4$.

This next problem has three parameters:

$$z = 2x_1 - x_2 + x_3 \qquad (2.5)$$

and three constraints:

$$3x_1 + x_2 + x_3 \le 60$$
$$x_1 - x_2 + 2x_3 \le 10 \qquad (2.6)$$
$$x_1 + x_2 - x_3 \le 20$$

The solution domain and values are shown in this next figure:

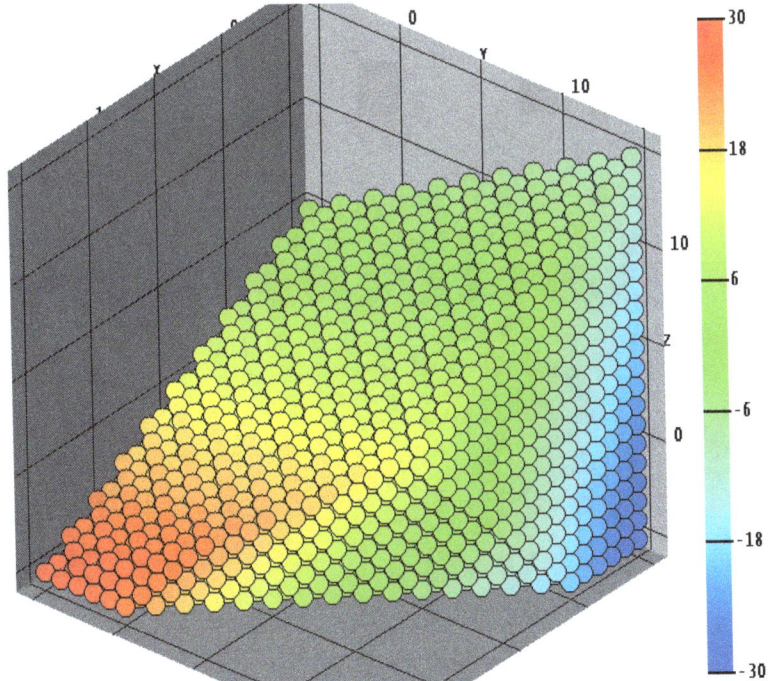

The optimum solution meeting the constraints is $z=25$ at $x_1=15$, $x_2=5$, $x_3=0$. We use the Excel™ Solver™ to find the solution. Before you can use this tool, you must enable it by checking the appropriate box, as shown in this next figure:

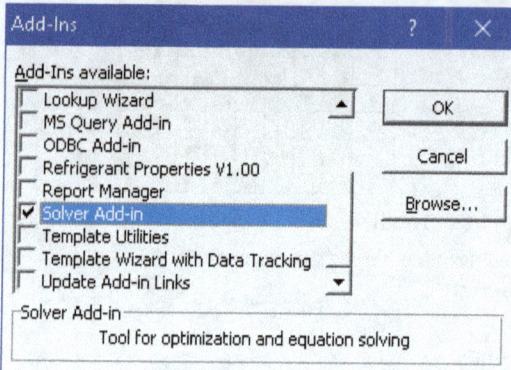

Figure 10. Enabling the Excel Solver Add-In

We set up the problem in a spreadsheet, as shown here:

	A	B
1	maximize:	
2	Z=2*x1-x2+x3	
3	x1=	15
4	x2=	5
5	x3=	0
6	Z=	25
7	subject to:	
8	3*x1+x2+x3≤60	50
9	x1-x2+2*x3≤10	10
10	x1+x2-x3≤20	20

Figure 11. Setting Up the Problem

with the solution in cells B3:B5. Then we pull up the Solver:

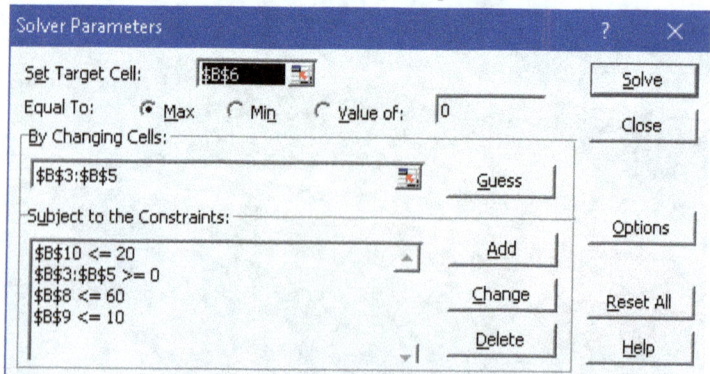

Figure 12. Defining the Problem

10

The cell to be maximized is called the "target" and is defined at the top. That we desire a maximal value is set just below this. We could also seek a minimum (such as cost or time to produce) or a specific value on this same line. The variables to be adjusted are shown below "By Changing Cells:". The constraints are entered in the bottom window. Press [Solve] and Excel will find the solution. The details are highlighted in this next figure:

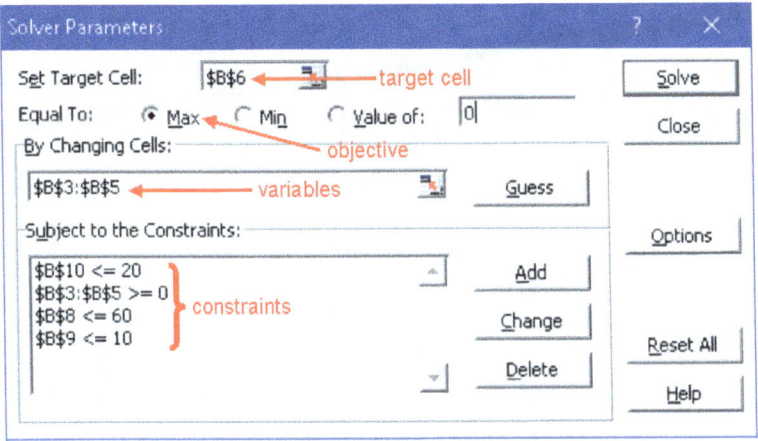

Figure 13. Solver Parameter Details

You can also set these parameters in a macro, as shown below:

```
Sub SetSolverOptions()
  Worksheets("Sheet1").Activate
  SolverReset
  SolverOptions Precision:=0.001
  SolverOK SetCell:=Range("TotalProfit"), _
    MaxMinVal:=1, _
    ByChange:=Range("C4:E6")
  SolverAdd CellRef:=Range("F4:F6"), _
    Relation:=1, _
    FormulaText:=100
  SolverAdd CellRef:=Range("C4:E6"), _
    Relation:=3, _
    FormulaText:=0
  SolverAdd CellRef:=Range("C4:E6"), _
    Relation:=4
  SolverSolve UserFinish:=False
  SolverSave SaveArea:=Range("A33")
End Sub
```

Two similar examples are shown in this next figure:

	A	B
1	minimize:	
2	Z=x1+2*x2	
3	x1=	15
4	x2=	30
5	Z=	75
6	subject to:	
7	-x1+x2≤15	15
8	2*x1+x2≤90	60
9	x2≥30	30
10	and:	
11	x1≥0	
12	x2≥0	

	A	B
1	maximize:	
2	Z=2*x1+2*x2+3*x3	
3	x1=	0
4	x2=	1.666667
5	x3=	2.333333
6	Z=	10.33333
7	subject to:	
8	2*x1+x2+2*x3≤4	4
9	x1+x2+x3≤3	3
10	and:	
11	x1≥0	
12	x2≥0	
13	x3≥0	

Figure 14. Two Similar Examples

12

Chapter 3. Nonlinear Examples

The examples in the preceding chapter were all linear. Many (if not most) process optimization problems are nonlinear or at least include nonlinear elements. We begin with a simple example:

$$z = 8x + 6y - 10 - x^2 - y^2 \qquad (3.1)$$

Excel readily calculates the values over a range of x and y:

	0	1	2	3	4	5	6	7
0	-10	-3	2	5	6	5	2	-3
1	-5	2	7	10	11	10	7	2
2	-2	5	10	13	14	13	10	5
3	-1	6	11	14	15	14	11	6
4	-2	5	10	13	14	13	10	5
5	-5	2	7	10	11	10	7	2
6	-10	-3	2	5	6	5	2	-3
7	-17	-10	-5	-2	-1	-2	-5	-10

Excel will draw and fill contours if the data are arranged in this 2D tabular form:

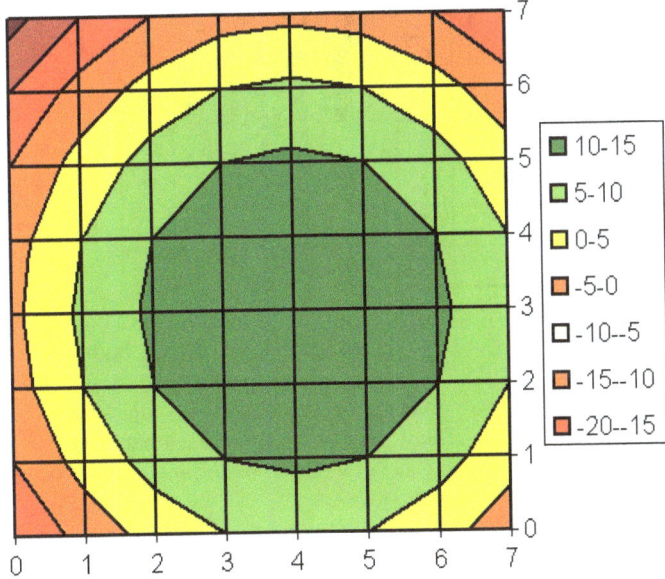

We see that the maximum (z=15) occurs at x=4, y=3. This particular problem is easily solved but we could use Excel's Solver, as before.

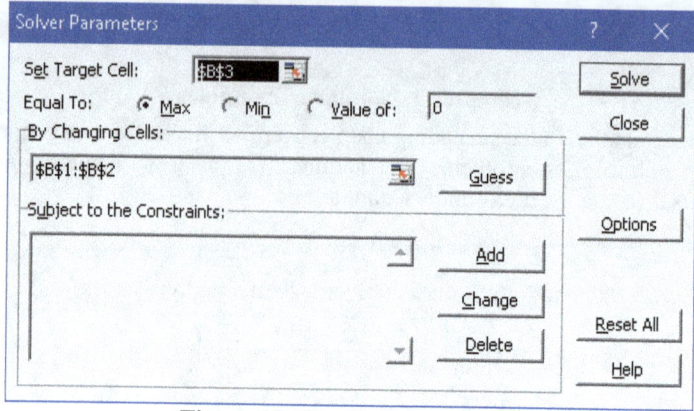

Figure 15. Excel's Solver Setup

We will need the Solver for more complex problems, but first we consider constraints, which are often found in manufacturing. What if y were cars and x were sunroofs? Not all cars have sunroofs but we certainly don't want more sunroofs than cars, so x≤y. We could add this constraint visually:

	0	1	2	3	4	5	6	7
0	-10	3	2	5	6	5	2	-3
1	-5	2	7	10	11	10	7	2
2	-2	5	10	13	14	13	10	5
3	-1	6	11	14	15	14	11	6
4	-2	5	10	13	14	13	10	5
5	-5	2	7	10	11	10	7	2
6	-10	-3	2	5	6	5	2	-3
7	-17	-10	-5	-2	-1	-2	-5	-10

This constraint eliminates the first solution and adds another complexity: There are now two solutions (x=3, y=3) and (x=4, y=4) which both yield the same result (z=14). This situation is also common in manufacturing: There may be two (or more) ways (or operations or procedures or adjustments) that yield essentially the same result. There may be no preference between these or there may be other factors, such as previous (or current operation) or which changeover is easiest (or fastest).

14

Multiple Highs or Lows

In real, practical problems we often see multiple highs (profit or items produced) or lows (cost or flaws). Sometimes these are obvious and sometimes not. Sometimes we can choose which one to aim for, while in other situations we cannot. Consider this next graphic:

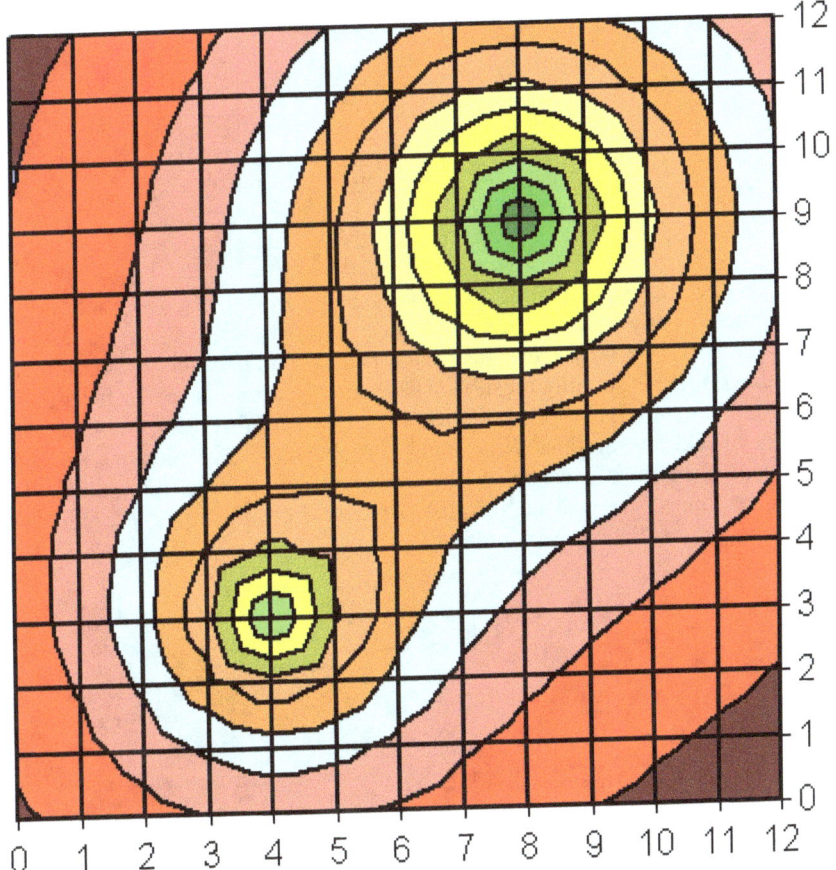

We could aim for x=4, y=3 or x=8, y=9. In this example we see two differences: 1) the center of the second target is greener (greater profit or more items produced) than the first target; and 2) the green area is larger around the second target (we would still remain profitable, even if we didn't reach the optimal point exactly or if our map doesn't precisely fit the process in question.

The table of value is shown in this next figure:

	A	B	C	D	E	F	G	H	I	J	K	L	M	N	O	P	Q
1	x	8			0	1	2	3	4	5	6	7	8	9	10	11	12
2	y	9		0	4	6	8	10	11	11	9	8	6	5	4	3	3
3	z	61		1	6	8	12	16	18	17	14	11	8	7	6	5	4
4				2	7	10	16	23	28	24	18	14	11	9	7	6	5
5				3	8	12	18	29	45	31	22	17	14	11	9	8	6
6				4	8	12	18	25	31	28	23	19	16	14	12	10	8
7				5	7	11	15	20	24	24	23	22	20	18	15	12	10
8				6	7	10	13	17	20	23	25	26	25	23	19	15	12
9				7	6	9	12	15	19	23	28	32	33	30	24	19	14
10				8	6	8	11	14	18	24	31	40	45	39	29	21	16
11				9	5	7	10	13	18	24	32	44	61	44	31	22	16
12				10	5	7	9	12	16	22	30	38	44	38	29	21	15
13				11	4	6	8	11	14	19	24	29	31	29	24	18	14
14				12	4	5	7	9	12	15	18	21	22	21	18	15	11

The Excel Solver will find x=8, y=9 but not if you begin at x=0, y=0 or many other starting value pairs, so you must "help" it along. This is because the algorithm merely follows the steepest ascent for maximum (or descent for minimum) from the starting location. The algorithm does not search for a *global* maximum (or minimum). This is why it can be helpful to plot the values and visually check the solution. When more variables are involved you will need more sophisticated software to produce a meaningful graphic; for example TP2 (available free at the web address listed below the Preface) or Tecplot™ (an excellent commercial software product).

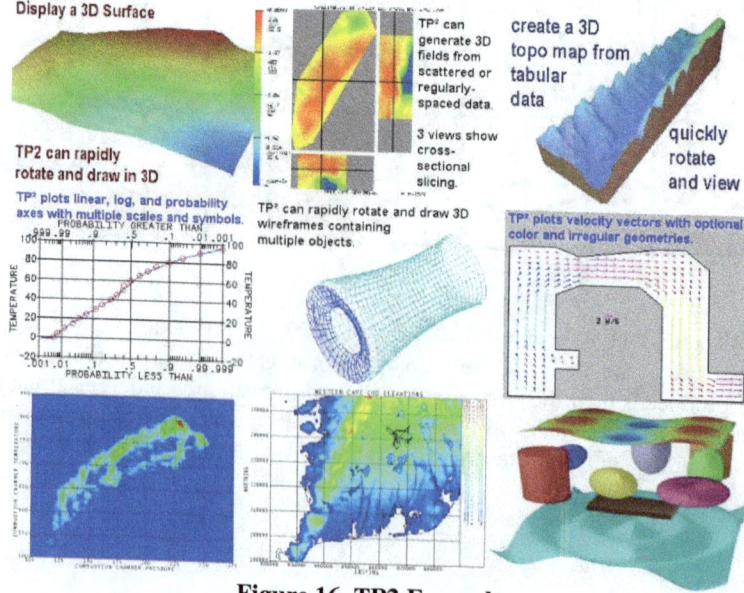

Figure 16. TP2 Examples

16

This next figure comes from a different field but is not unlike some industrial processes:

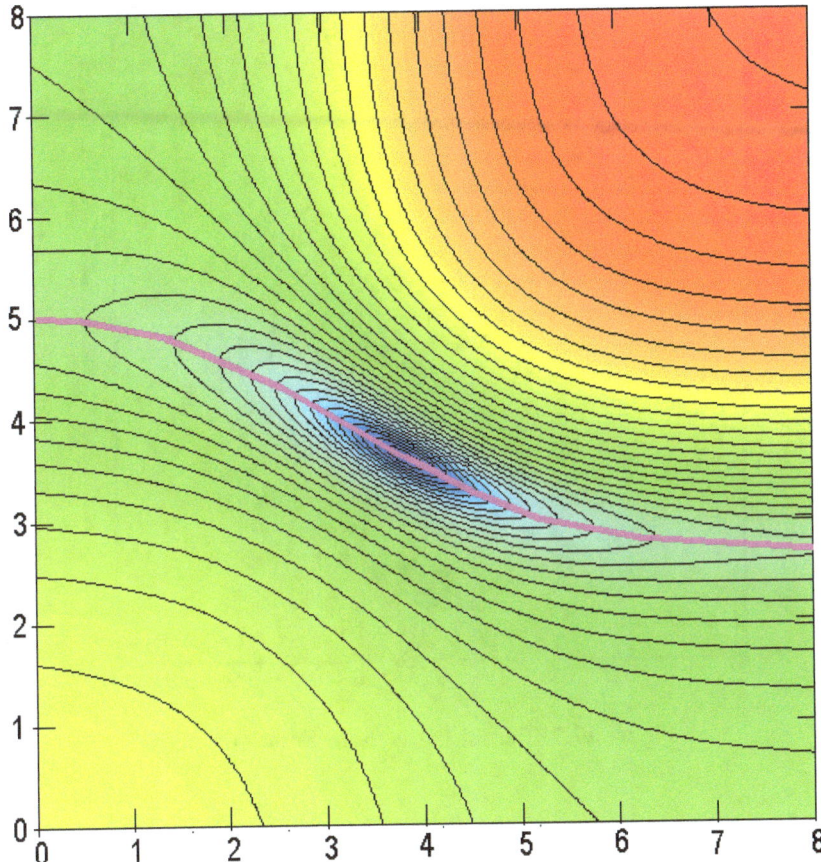

While the optimum (blue spot) is at about x=4, y=4, we could operate over the entire magenta curve from x=0, y=5 to x=8, y=3 and stay profitable or within the tolerable range of flaws. Finding the precise optimum in such a case would require a more sophisticated algorithm, which are beyond the scope of this text but are readily available elsewhere.

This next example illustrates an important concept: the path to the optimum point often depends on where you begin the process:

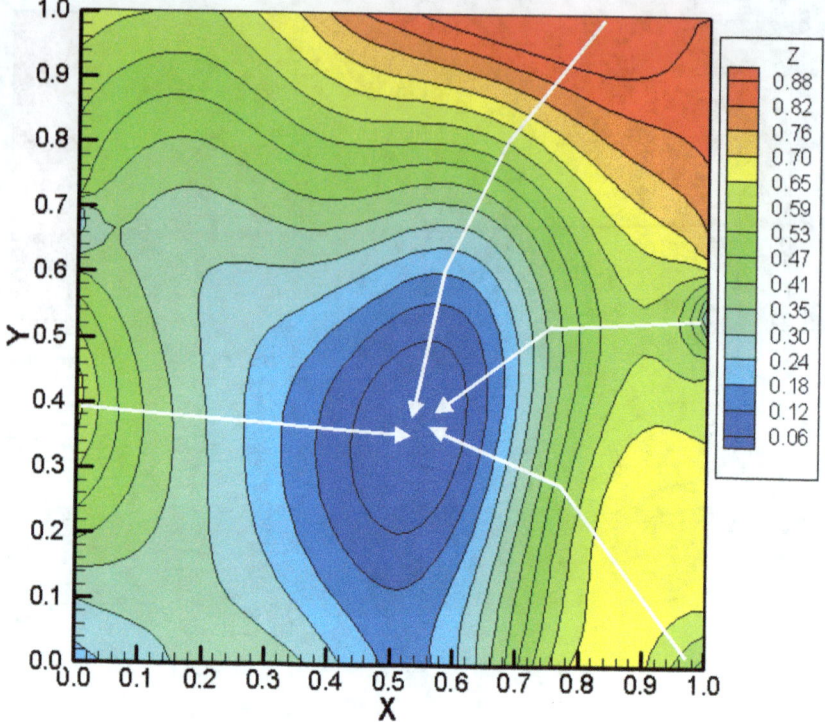

Figure 17. Different Paths to the Same Optimum

Chapter 4. Incorporating Calculus

Process metrics come in a wide variety of form and detail; for example, we might have data for the rate of production. If the rate of production rises and falls with some external factor over which we have no control (e.g., the weather, traffic, or availability of a key ingredient) and we desire the maximum total output, we would need to integrate the metric and find the maximum.

Suppose the workforce at your factory arrive hung over, resentful for having to work on New Year's Day. After consuming copious amounts of coffee, production rate reaches 100% at 10:00 AM, but falls off rapidly as lunchtime approaches. After consuming even more coffee, production again reaches 100% at 2:00 PM but this is not sustainable so that production falls off again. About 4:00 PM you offer a proposal: If they reach a modified goal by 5:00 PM, they can come in one hour late tomorrow. These metrics might look like the following:

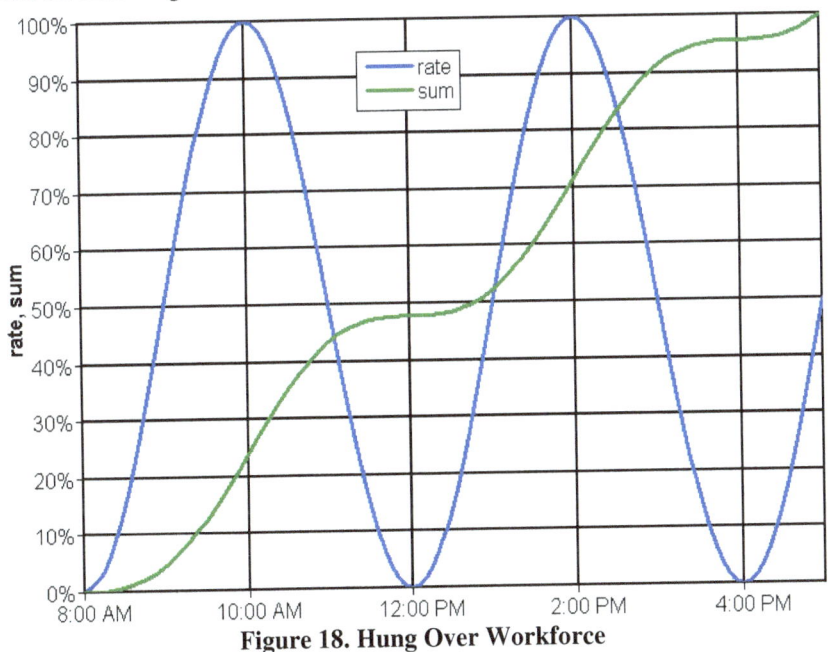

Figure 18. Hung Over Workforce

The blue rate curve is sin²(t). The green curve is the integral of this with respect to time or $\int \sin^2(t)dt = t/2 - \sin(2t)/4$. In order to illustrate this concept, we

19

consider an example using more familiar quantities: acceleration, velocity, and distance—all linked together by integration and differentiation.

Problem 1. Racecar

Suppose you are testing a racecar at the Bonneville Salt Flats, hoping to set a new world land speed record. For the first 60 seconds, the acceleration in ft/sec² is given by the following equation:

$$a = 30\frac{(60-t)^2}{60^2} = \frac{t^2}{120} - t + 30 \tag{4.1}$$

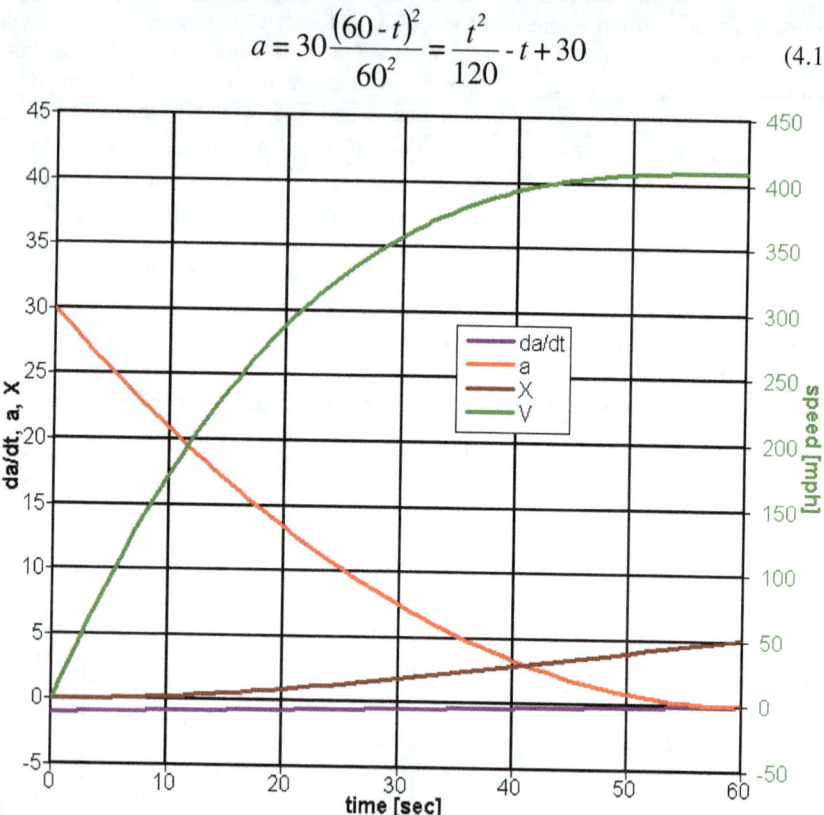

Figure 19. Racecar Metrics

We integrate this equation with respect to time in order to arrive at an expression for the velocity in ft/sec:

$$V = \int_0^t a\,dt = \frac{t^3}{360} - \frac{t^2}{2} + 30t \tag{4.2}$$

We integrate again with respect to time in order to arrive at an expression for the position in ft:

20

$$X = \int_0^t V dt = \frac{t^4}{1440} - \frac{t^3}{6} + 15t^2 \qquad (4.3)$$

We can differentiate Equation 4.1 to obtain an expression for the rate of change of acceleration in ft/sec³:

$$\frac{da}{dt} = \frac{t}{60} - 1 \qquad (4.4)$$

The corresponding curves are shown in the preceding figure. The maximum acceleration is 30 ft/sec² and occurs at t=0. The minimum acceleration is zero and occurs at t=60 sec. The maximum velocity is 409 mph and also occurs at t=60. The distance covered in 60 seconds is 5.11 miles. The most convenient way to solve and graph this process is in an Excel™ spreadsheet, which can be found in the online archive accompanying this text at the web address listed in the Preface.

One convenient feature of such a spreadsheet will allow us to calculate when the speed reaches 60 mph. We select cell D6 and pull up the Solver, which must be enabled as an Add-In if you haven't already done so. We want this cell to equal 60 by adjusting the time in cell A6. The Solver tab will look like this:

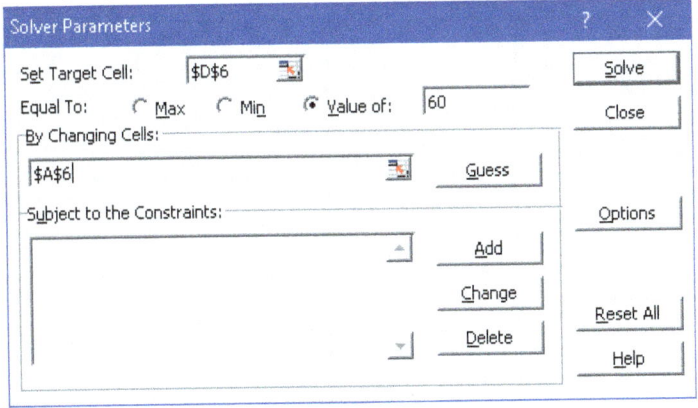

Figure 20. Excel Solver Add-In

The result is 3.09 seconds. We could have solved Equation 4.2 algebraically, which yields one real and two imaginary roots. The real root is given by:

$$t_{60} = 60 - 16(45)^{\frac{1}{3}} = 3.089707... \qquad (4.5)$$

In this first problem we performed sequential integrations to obtain the desired relationships. In this next problem we will use sequential derivatives.

Problem 2. Elevator Drop

We present this problem as the elevator drop ride at an amusement park but it might as well be the position of an extrusion press squashing out charcoal grills or patio furniture, as the calculus is the same. The position is given by:

$$z = \frac{g\,t^2}{2}\left(\frac{t^3}{20} - 1\right) + h \tag{4.6}$$

The process lasts 2 seconds and g=9.81 m/s². We first calculate the drop, h, by substituting z=0 at t=2 and solving for h, which yields: 11.8 meters. The speed (velocity) is found by taking the derivative with respect to time:

$$V = \frac{dz}{dt} = gt\left(\frac{t^3}{8} - 1\right) \tag{4.7}$$

The acceleration is equal to the second derivative with respect to time:

$$a = \frac{dV}{dt} = \frac{g}{2}\left(t^3 - 2\right) \tag{4.8}$$

The position, velocity, and acceleration are shown below:

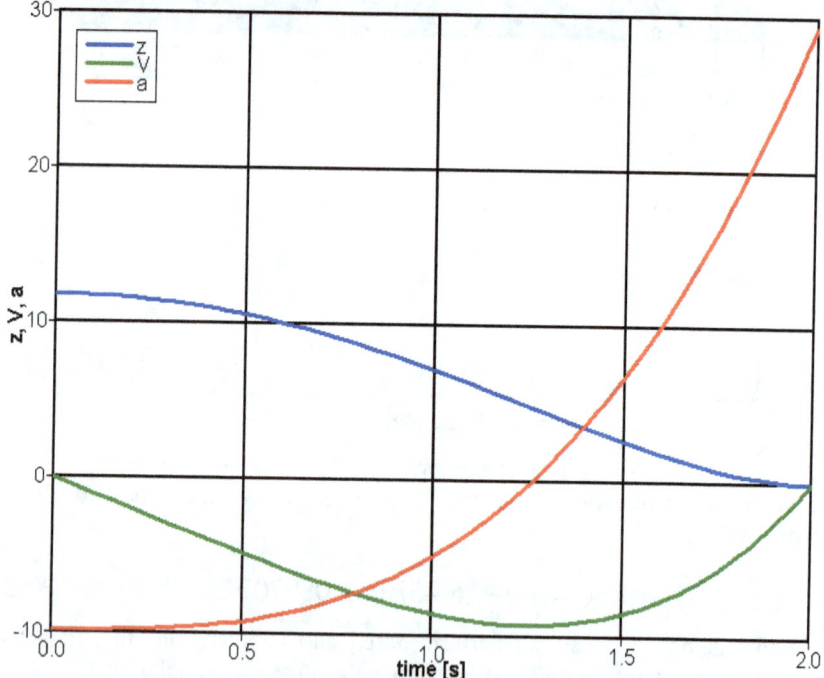

Figure 21. Elevator Drop

The maximum downward acceleration is -9.81 m/s², which occurs at t=0. The maximum upward acceleration is +29.43 m/s², which occurs at t=2, as the ride reaches the bottom (z=0). This is equivalent to 3 g's (i.e., three times the acceleration of gravity). We can use the Excel Solver to find the time and location of maximum velocity.

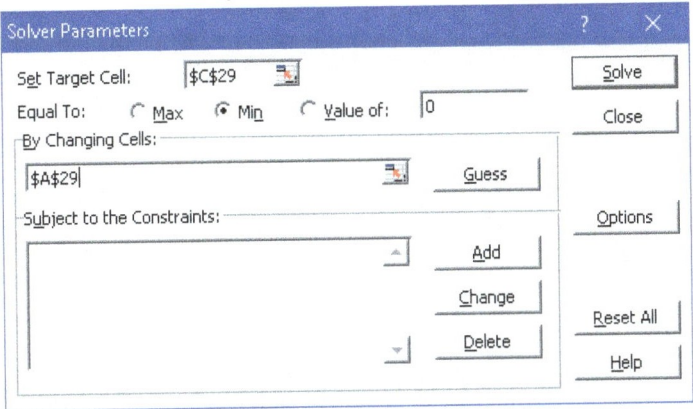

Figure 22. Excel Solver

We set the target to cell C29, click (•) next to Min to find the largest negative velocity, by adjusting the time in cell A29. The result is -9.27 m/s at 1.26 sec and an elevation of 4.76 m. As before, we could solve for this analytically, but Excel is convenient, fast, and works for very complex equations as well as empirical data that may not be provided in the form of an equation.

Gradients

Many problems have more than one variable. When we seek to find the minimum (or maximum) of cost (or output) in such cases we need *directional derivatives* (or slopes). The mathematical term for these is *gradients*. The concept is familiar, though perhaps not in this context. We might notice, for example, that the likelihood of flaws varies with the time of day, perhaps linked to attention and fatigue. We may further notice that the frequency of flaws varies with noise level. If we have a particularly critical product for which minimizing flaws is of great importance, we might seek that combination of time of day and noise most conducive to achieving that goal. We could create a map from past experience based on each time a flaw occurred. We might search the map to find the best conditions. Conceptually, this is no different from finding the lowest elevation on a topographic map. Water naturally flows *down gradient*, which is where the mathematical term originates. The shortest route from where we are to the bottom can be indicated by little arrows on the map. Following these paths achieves a *steepest descent*, which is what we call the mathematical algorithm inspired by this concept, presented in a subsequent chapter. A typical

23

topographic map with elevation contours and arrows showing the way down from each location is illustrated in the following figure:

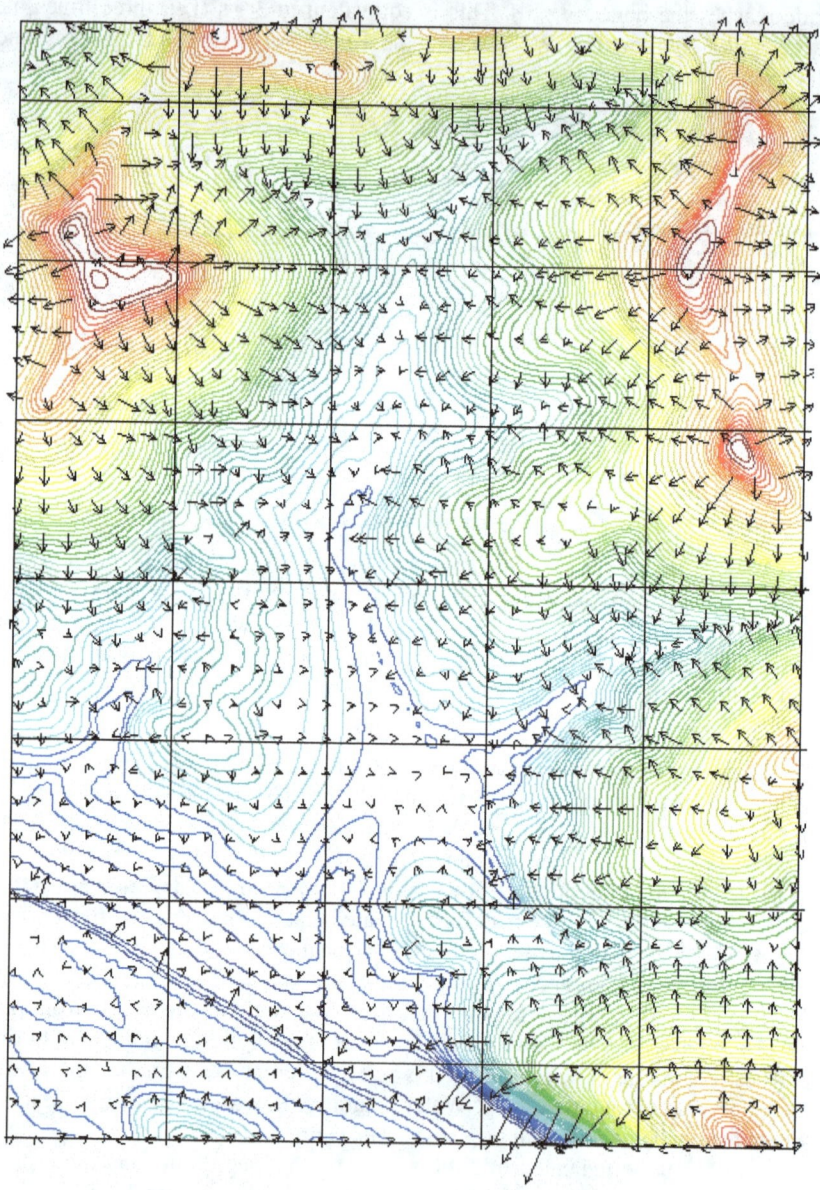

Figure 23. Topographic Map with Down Gradient Vectors

Braking

According to EuroTrans it takes a typical auto traveling at a rate of 100 kilometers per hour 60 meters to halt on the typical European highway. What coefficient of friction between the tires and road does this imply? In order to solve this problem we must recall the relationship between force and acceleration, or Newton's First Law:

$$F = ma = m\frac{dV}{dt} = mV\frac{dV}{dx} \qquad (4.9)$$

where F is the force, a is the acceleration, V is the velocity, and t is time. The last two terms arise from the Chain Rule of Calculus. We can integrate this expression to find the work required to stop the vehicle, which is equal to the kinetic energy:

$$KE = \int_0^x Fdx = Fx = \int_0^x mV\frac{dV}{dx} = \frac{mV^2}{2} \qquad (4.10)$$

Here we have presumed the force to be constant over the braking process. The braking force is equal to the weight, W, times the coefficient of friction, f. The weight is equal to the mass, m, times the acceleration of gravity, g.

$$F = fW = fmg \qquad (4.11)$$

If the force is constant, then the acceleration will be constant (Equation 4.9), so that we have:

$$\frac{F}{m} = a = fg \qquad (4.12)$$

Combining 4.10 and 4.12 we get:

$$f = \frac{V^2}{2gx} \qquad (4.13)$$

Substituting the values yields the solution:

$$f = \frac{\left[\left(100\frac{km}{hr}\right)\left(1000\frac{m}{km}\right)\right]^2}{2\left(9.81\frac{m}{sec^2}\right)\left(3600\frac{sec}{hr}\right)^2(60m)} = 0.655 \qquad (4.14)$$

Turning

Another important aspect of moving equipment and machinery is angular momentum, which must be controlled and considered so that unexpected failures do not occur. Consider the following... A 3600-pound car rounds a 200-foot radius curve at 30 mph.

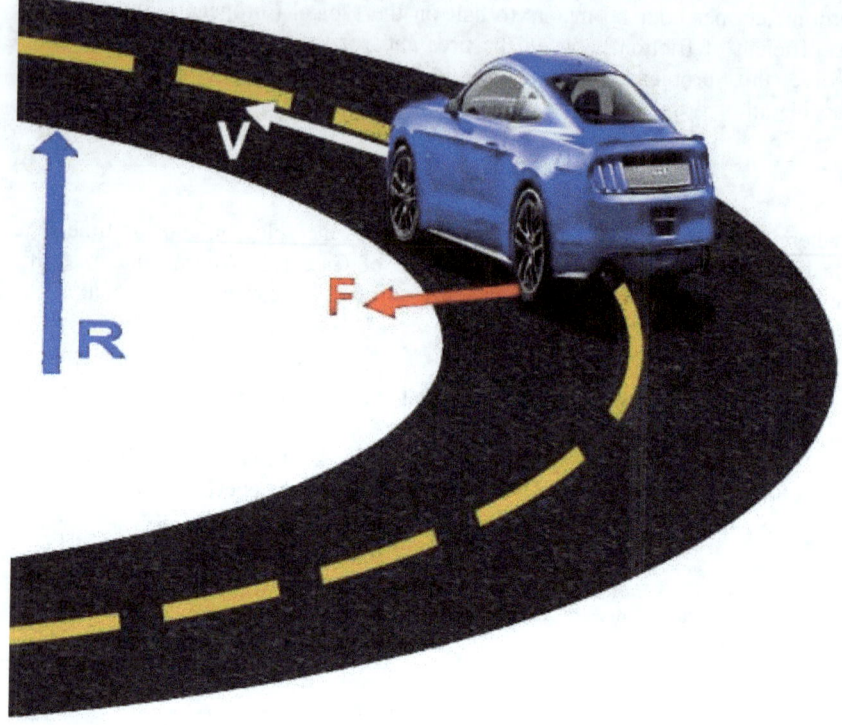

Figure 24. Car in Bend

What is the angular momentum of the car in ft-lbf-seconds as it reaches the middle of the bend? In the case the linear momentum is given by:

$$L = mVr \tag{4.15}$$

where L is the linear momentum, m is the mass, V is the velocity, and r is the radius. Substituting along with unit conversions gives:

$$L = \left[\frac{(3600\,lbm)}{\left(32.174\dfrac{lbm-ft}{lbf-sec^2}\right)}\right]\left[\frac{\left(30\dfrac{miles}{hr}\right)\left(5280\dfrac{ft}{mile}\right)}{\left(3600\dfrac{sec}{hr}\right)}\right](200\,ft) \tag{4.16}$$

$$= 984{,}646\,ft \cdot lbf \cdot sec$$

The denominator in the first term (32.174 lbm-ft/lbf-sec^2) is called Newton's constant and given the symbol, g_C. When working with English (i.e., U.S. Customary) units it is essential to distinguish between pounds mass (designated lbm) and pounds force (designated lbf). Note that one pound mass on the surface of the Earth weighs one pound force; whereas, one kg mass on the surface of the Earth weighs 9.81 Newtons. Note that while metric scales might display kilograms, they *do not* measure mass, rather they measure weight and display this value divided by 9.81.

What is the lateral acceleration of the car in g's (i.e., compared to the acceleration of gravity on the surface of the Earth)? The lateral (i.e., centripetal) acceleration in a curve is given by:

$$a = \frac{V^2}{r} \tag{4.17}$$

Substituting the values along with unit conversions yields:

$$a = \frac{\left[\left(30\frac{miles}{hr}\right)\left(5280\frac{ft}{mile}\right)\right]^2}{\left(3600\frac{sec}{hr}\right)} = 9.68\frac{ft}{sec^2} = 0.3g \tag{4.18}$$

What is the lateral force on the tires?

$$F = ma = (0.3)(3600) = 1083 lbf \tag{4.19}$$

Impact

Industrial processes may include some sort of impact, which we approximate as a falling object so as to quantify the effect. For example: if a one-pound weight falls ten feet to the floor, the energy absorbed by the impact will be ten ft-lbf (foot pounds force). We can convert this to SI units knowing that:

1 ft-lbf = 1.355817948 joule

so that the energy associated with one-pound object falling ten feet will be 13.56 joule. One joule is equal to one watt-second. We rarely use the joule or watt-second units. More often in SI units we use kilowatt-hour (kw-hr or kwh). As there are 1000 watts per kilowatt and 3600 seconds per hour, there are 3,600,000 joules per kwh. The ft-lbf unit is also uncommon. More often in English (or U.S. Customary) units we use the British Thermal Unit (or BTU), which is a measure of heat and also energy.

1 BTU = 1055.055853 joule

The more common relationship for this conversion is:

27

$$1 \text{ kwh} = 3412.141633 \text{ BTU}$$

If the 3600-pound car slams into a wall at 30 mph, the energy involved is obtained using Equation 4.10:

$$KE = \frac{mV^2}{2} = \frac{(3600lbm)}{\left(32.174\dfrac{lbm-ft}{lbf-sec^2}\right)}\left[\frac{\left(30\dfrac{mile}{hr}\right)\left(5280\dfrac{ft}{mile}\right)}{\left(3600\dfrac{sec}{hr}\right)}\right]^2 \quad (4.20)$$

$$= 216,622\,ft \cdot lbf = 278.4\,BTU = 0.08158\,kw \cdot hr$$

In this example we see that the BTU is much larger (1055x) than the ft-lbf and the kwh is much larger (3412x) than the BTU. This example helps put things into perspective, considering that the average cost of electricity in the U.S. is 17¢/kwh. In order to reach 1 kwh, our 3600-pound car would have to smash into the wall at 105 mph.

Optimum 100-Yard Dash

How fast should you run in the rain so as to get the least wet?

Figure 25. Running in the Rain

28

To solve this problem we will approximate the runner as a cylinder:

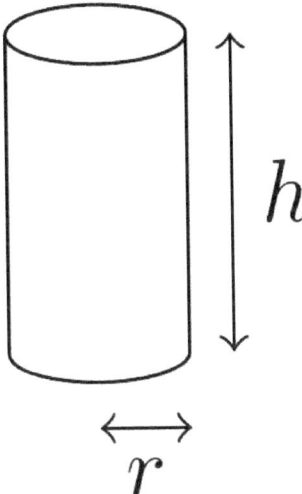

Figure 26. Cylinder

of height, h, and radius, r. We will also assume that the rain falls vertically downward. The vertical area of this cylinder is $A_V = \pi r^2$. The horizontal area of this cylinder is $A_H = 2rh$. The distance covered is, d, and equal to 300 feet. The time to run (cover the required distance) is t in seconds. The rate of rainfall we give the symbol w in drops per square foot per second. The speed at which droplets fall we give the symbol f in feet per second. The speed at which the runner moves through the rain is given the symbol v in feet per second. The time required is then equal to $t = d/v$.

The number of drops falling from the top on to the runner is equal to the vertical area times the rainfall rate times the duration of the run or:

$$n_V = A_V wt \qquad (4.21)$$

The number of drops encountered by running (sideways) through the rain is given by:

$$n_H = A_V \left(\frac{w}{f}\right) d \left(\frac{v}{\sqrt{f^2 + v^2}}\right) \qquad (4.22)$$

which is the horizontal projected area times the ratio of the rainfall density to downward velocity times the distance times the ratio of the horizontal to vertical right triangle (Pythagorean theorem) proportion of the volume the runner sweeps through the rain.

The spreadsheet (raindash.xls) looks like this:

	A	B	C	D	E	F	G
1			optimal 100-yard dash in the rain				
2	rain flux	100	drop/ft²/sec	speed	top drops	side drops	total drops
3	rain fall	10	ft/sec	1	94,248	3,582	97,830
4	radius	1	ft	2	47,124	7,060	54,184
5	height	6	ft	3	31,416	10,345	41,760
6	top area	3.14	ft²	4	23,562	13,370	36,932
7	side area	12	ft²	5	18,850	16,100	34,949
8	fall time	0.6	sec	6	15,708	18,522	34,230
9	distance	300	ft	6.81	13,843	20,260	34,103
10	run speed	5	ft/sec	7	13,464	20,645	34,109
11	run time	60	sec	8	11,781	22,489	34,270
12	top drops	18,850	drops	9	10,472	24,083	34,555
13	side drops	16,100	drops	10	9,425	25,456	34,881
14	total drops	34,949	drops				

Figure 27. Rain Dash Spreadsheet

The left side is one particular solution based on running at a rate of 5 ft/sec. The right side is a table of v=1 to 10, which is shown in this figure:

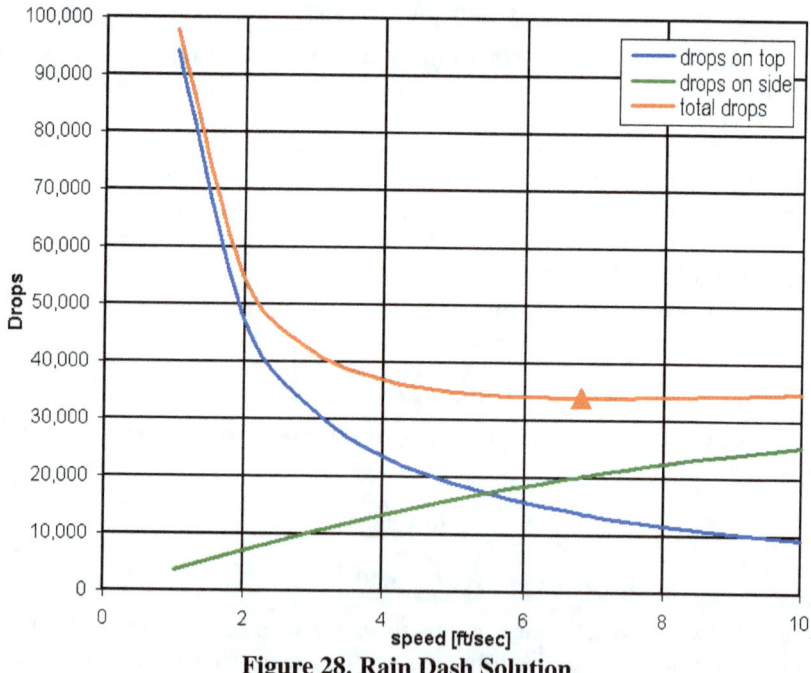

Figure 28. Rain Dash Solution

We can use the Solver to locate the optimum (minimize cell G9 by changing D9), which is 6.81 ft/sec.

30

Best RPM To Shift

In this example we consider at what rpm (engine speed) is it best to shift (up to the next gear in order to achieve the fastest quarter mile time)? In order to do this we will have to bring together several things: basic equations of motion, empirical data for resistance, property formulas, unit conversions, gear ratios, and calculus plus a few spreadsheet tricks and Excel's Solver. All the details may be found in spreadsheet car.xls in the online archive. First we consider the engine performance, which is shown in this first figure:

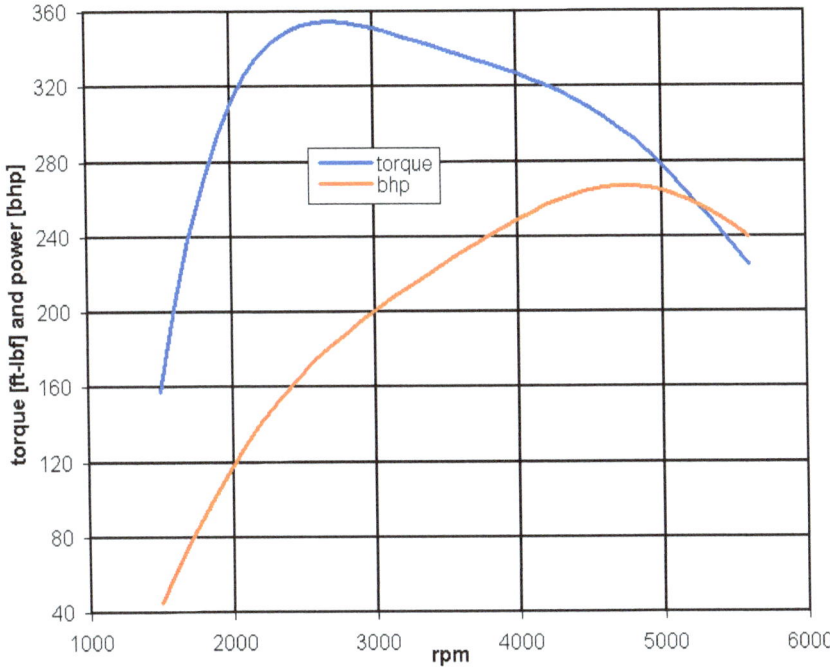

Figure 29. Typical Engine Curves

The orange (torque) curve was digitized and curve-fitted. The freebie curve-fitting program (Curvefit) provides the Excel macro, which has been rearranged with parentheses for compactness:

```
Function Torque(rpm As Double) As Double
   Torque = ((((2.84375216025E-15 * rpm
      - 5.88763420508E-11) * rpm _
      + 4.75414739036E-07) * rpm _
      - 0.00188319233776) * rpm _
      + 3.65009513779) * rpm - 2408.55743668
End Function
```

The power curve is calculated because power is equal to torque times rotational speed in radians (there are 2π radians in one rotation). The code is:

31

```
Const Pi As Double = 3.14159265358979
Function Horsepower(rpm As Double) As Double
   Horsepower = rpm * Torque(rpm) * (2 * Pi) / 550 / 60
End Function
```

where 550 is the conversion from bhp (brake horsepower) to ft-lbf/sec (foot-pounds force per second) and 60 is the conversion from minutes to seconds. Note that torque is in foot-lbf (foot-pounds force). We next consider resistance, which is in two parts: rolling and form drag. Rolling resistance arises from several factors, including constant deforming of the tires. This is most often approximated as a constant times the weight of the car or:

$$F_R = C_R W \qquad (4.23)$$

Typical values of C_R range from 0.005 to 0.025. Here we will use 0.010 for this example. We will use a weight of 3600 pounds. Next is the form drag (i.e., wind resistance). This is most often approximated by a coefficient times the frontal (projected) area times the dynamic pressure, which is equal to the density times the velocity squared divided by 2. When using English (i.e., U.S. customary) units it is necessary to include Newton's constant, g_C, which is equal to 32.174 lbm-ft/lbf/sec² (pounds mass foot per pound force second squared). [The SI equivalent is 1 kg-m/N/s² or one kilogram meter per Newton per second squared].

$$F_D = C_D A_P \frac{\rho V^2}{2 g_C} \qquad (4.24)$$

The density of air can be calculated with adequate accuracy using the ideal gas law, which is:

$$\rho = \frac{p}{RT} \qquad (4.25)$$

where ρ is the density in lbm/ft³ (pounds mass per cubic foot), p is the pressure in psia (pounds force per square inch absolute), R is the ideal gas constant, and T is the absolute temperature in °R (degrees Rankine). The ideal gas constant in English (i.e., U.S. customary) units is equal to 1545.348 ft-lbf/°R/lb-mole (foot pounds force per degree Rankine per pound mole). This must be divided by the molecular weight of air, which is 28.966. We must also multiply pressure time 144 in²/ft² (inches squared per foot squared) for the units to come out right. When using temperature in °F (degrees Fahrenheit) we must add 459.67 to get °F. At 70°F and standard atmospheric pressure at sea level (14.696 psia) the density of air is about 0.07489 lbm/ft³ (pounds mass per cubic foot).

We combine all of these to get the rolling, form, and total resistance, which is shown in this next figure:

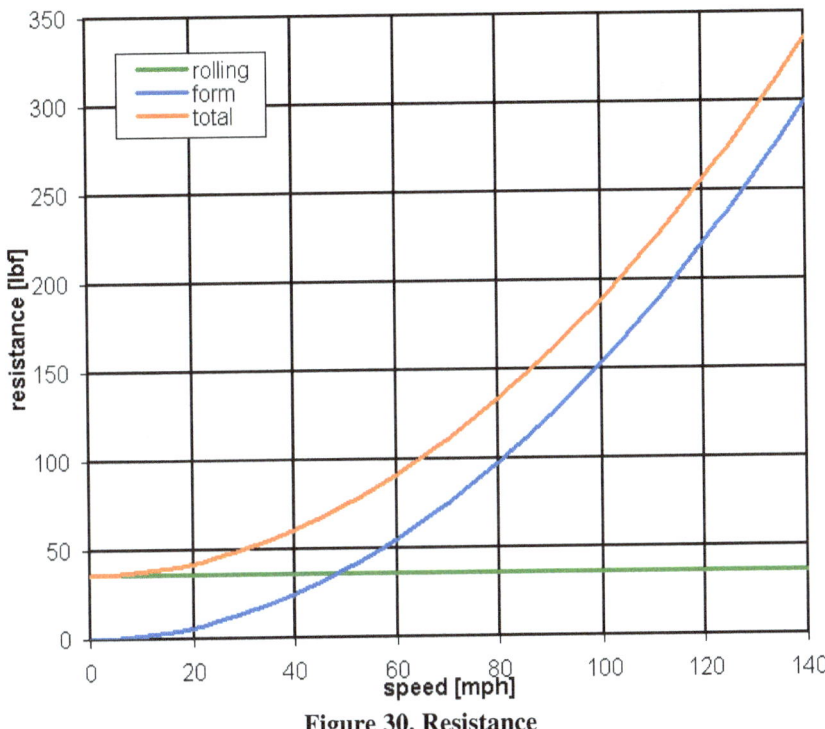

Figure 30. Resistance

We next consider gears, which include the transmission and rear axle. Linking the forward speed of the car to the rotational of speed of the engine also requires the diameter of the tires under load. To simplify this we will assume no slip (in the gear train) and constant deformation of the tires so that we arrive at simple linear relationships. Typical gear ratios for a 4-speed transmission are:

gear ratios	
1st	4.00
2nd	2.52
3rd	1.59
4th	1.00
final	40.00

This gives us the following relationships for vehicle (translational) speed vs. engine (rotational) speed for each gear:

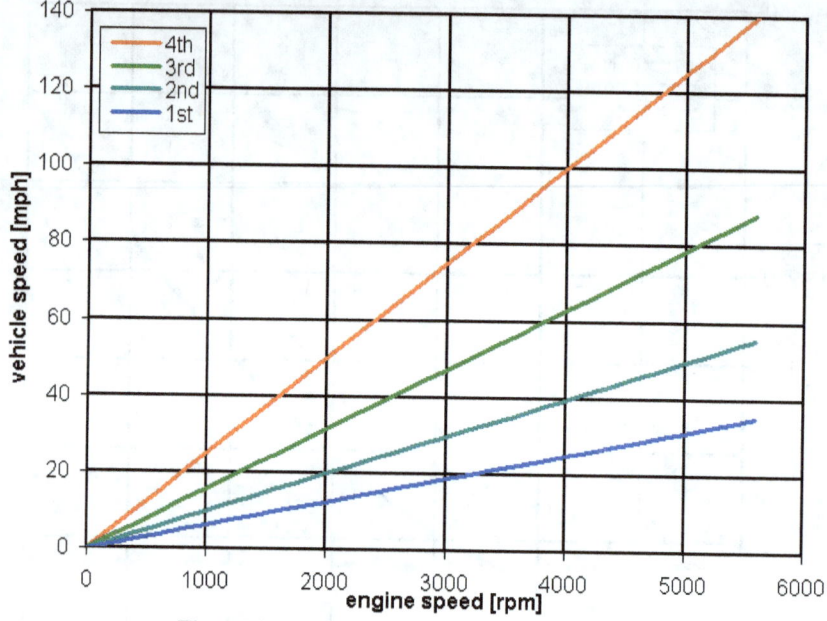

Figure 31. Vehicle to Engine Speed by Gear

We can see how this might be any number of industrial processes, which in order to analyze, we must gather various types of information and pull together principles and properties from multiple disciplines so as to build a realistic model that lends itself to mathematical manipulation and ultimately optimization. We next must deal with the calculus. First, we have Newton's second law (force is equal to mass times acceleration):

$$a = \frac{dv}{dt} = \frac{g_C F}{m} \tag{4.26}$$

where a is the acceleration, equal to the derivative of velocity, v, with respect to time, t, F is the force, m is the mass, and g_C is Newton's constant. For example, a force of 300 lbf (pounds force) will accelerate a 3600 lbm (pound mass) car at a rate of 2.68 ft/sec.

$$a = \frac{\left(\dfrac{32.174\,lbm - ft}{lbf - \sec^2}\right)(300\,lbf)}{(3600\,lbm)} = 2.68\frac{ft}{\sec^2} \tag{4.27}$$

34

We must next select a method to step through time. Mathematically, this is integration:

$$v = \int_0^t a \cdot dt$$
$$x = \int_0^t v \cdot dt \qquad (4.28)$$

The simplest approximation is called the *Forward Euler* method. This will be adequate for our purpose here, as long as we use small time steps. This can be expressed as follows:

$$v_{t+\Delta t} = v_t + a_t \Delta t$$
$$x_{t+\Delta t} = x_t + v_t \Delta t \qquad (4.29)$$

Here's a challenge... In order to get this process started, we must assume some level of slip, whether in a clutch (for a manual transmission) or a torque converter (for an automatic transmission) or between the tires and the road; because the car begins at zero velocity and the engine cannot slow to zero rpm. We pick some reasonable minimum rpm (say 2000), which in traditional drag racing is called the *stall*. This will be a user input in the spreadsheet.

We next build the car motion calculations into the spreadsheet on the simulation tab. The first calculation in this process is calculating the forward thrust (force) applied by the engine through the tires to the road. This is equal to the torque times the final gear ratio including tire diameter plus conversion factors. For example:

$$F = 2\pi \frac{\left(311\,ft - lbf\right)\left(\dfrac{160\,rpm}{mph}\right)\left(\dfrac{60\,min}{hr}\right)}{\left(\dfrac{5280\,ft}{mile}\right)} = 3553\,lbf \qquad (4.30)$$

We subtract the resistance (rolling + form drag, which at $v=0$ is 36 lbf) to get the net force, then calculate the acceleration using Equation 4.26; for example:

$$a = \frac{\left(3517\,lbf\right)\left(32.174\,\dfrac{lbm - ft}{lbf - sec^2}\right)\left(\dfrac{3600\,sec}{hr}\right)}{\left(3600\,lbm\right)\left(\dfrac{5280\,ft}{mile}\right)} = 21.65\,\frac{mph}{sec} \qquad (4.31)$$

We create a spreadsheet to implement these calculations (car.xls) which begins with a column of time in seconds and a column containing the gear (1 through 4). At each time we must calculate the drive ratio (a numerical value representing the mechanical connection between the engine and the forward motion of the car), the engine speed (rpm), the torque, the resistance (rolling + form drag), the net effective force of the wheels on the pavement, the resulting acceleration (in mph/sec), velocity (speed in mph), and distance traveled (in feet). We need the velocity in order to calculate the rpm and the drag, hence the acceleration. We need the acceleration to calculate the velocity, which raises a conflict: If you input a circular calculation (i.e., one that references itself, even if indirectly through several other calculations), you will get an error like this:

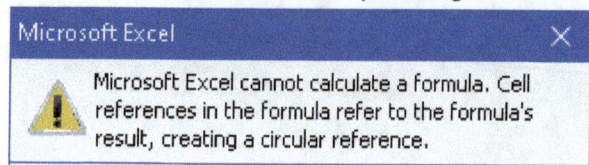

Figure 32. Circular Reference Error

In order to avoid this problem, we must carefully select which cell we use to create each formula. We begin at $t=v=x=0$. At $t=\Delta t$ we can use the velocity at $t=0$ to calculate the rpm, drag, net force, and acceleration. We then step along in time until the rpm reaches the shift point, which is a user input we define in a cell. It takes a finite amount of time to shift gears (whether manually or automatically) and so this is also a user input defined in a cell. When we reach the first shift point, we step forward in time by this amount, during which interval there is no force from the engine but there is still drag so that the acceleration is slightly negative. The velocity will decrease slightly during the shift interval.

We must divide the simulation up into four intervals, one for each gear. The first interval begins at rest in first gear and continues until reaching the shift point, at which time the engine disconnects, the acceleration briefly goes negative, and the car keeps rolling. After the shift interval we move to second gear and continue until the shift point is again reached, and so forth for third and fourth gear. To distinguish between the four segments we can use different highlight colors.

There is another challenge... How many cells does it take (i.e., how many time steps) to span each gear? We can't have a variable number of rows in a spreadsheet (i.e., the number of rows can't be a variable that changes with the other parameters as we run through the simulation). Therefore, we must change the time step during each gear so as to cover the necessary rpm in the number of cells chosen. In this case we pick 21 cells per gear. This means that we must adjust the time step in each gear so that after 20 steps, we reach the shift rpm. We must, therefore create four more variables, which must be adjusted each time we run the simulation or we won't reach the shift point at the specified rpm.

The simulation looks like this:

	A	B	C	D	E	F	G	H	I	J
1				time step simulation using forward Euler						
2	t	tran	drive	eng	torq	R	F	a	v	x
3	sec	gear	ratio	rpm	ft-lbf	lbf	lbf	mph/sec	mph	ft
4	0.00	1	160	2,000	311	36	3519	21.44	0	0
5	0.06	1	160	2,000	311	36	3519	21.44	1	0
6	0.12	1	160	2,000	311	36	3519	21.44	3	0
7	0.18	1	160	2,000	311	36	3518	21.44	4	1
8	0.23	1	160	2,000	311	36	3518	21.44	5	1
9	0.29	1	160	2,000	311	37	3518	21.44	6	2
10	0.35	1	160	2,000	311	37	3518	21.44	8	2
11	0.41	1	160	2,000	311	37	3518	21.43	9	3
12	0.47	1	160	2,000	311	38	3517	21.43	10	4
13	0.53	1	160	2,000	311	38	3517	21.43	11	5
14	0.59	1	160	2,009	313	38	3532	21.52	13	6
15	0.64	1	160	2,210	337	39	3817	23.26	14	7
16	0.70	1	160	2,428	351	40	3968	24.18	15	8
17	0.76	1	160	2,655	355	40	4014	24.46	17	10
18	0.82	1	160	2,884	353	41	3995	24.34	18	11
19	0.88	1	160	3,112	349	42	3944	24.03	19	13
20	0.94	1	160	3,337	344	43	3882	23.65	21	15
21	1.00	1	160	3,559	338	44	3819	23.27	22	17
22	1.05	1	160	3,777	333	45	3757	22.89	24	19
23	1.11	1	160	3,991	327	46	3692	22.50	25	21
24	**1.17**	1	160	**4,202**	**321**	47	**3618**	**22.05**	26	23
25	**1.67**					47	-47	-0.28	26	42
26	1.73	2	101	2,633	355	46	2507	15.28	26	45
27	1.78	2	101	2,720	355	47	2507	15.28	27	47
28	1.84	2	101	2,807	354	48	2502	15.24	28	49
29	1.90	2	101	2,893	353	49	2493	15.19	29	51
30	1.95	2	101	2,980	352	49	2481	15.12	30	54
31	2.01	2	101	3,066	350	50	2468	15.04	30	56
32	2.07	2	101	3,151	348	51	2453	14.95	31	59
33	2.12	2	101	3,236	346	52	2438	14.86	32	62
34	2.18	2	101	3,321	344	53	2422	14.76	33	64
35	2.24	2	101	3,405	342	53	2407	14.67	34	67
36	2.29	2	101	3,488	340	54	2391	14.57	35	70
37	2.35	2	101	3,571	338	55	2376	14.48	35	73
38	2.40	2	101	3,654	336	56	2361	14.38	36	76
39	2.46	2	101	3,735	334	57	2345	14.29	37	79
40	2.52	2	101	3,817	332	58	2330	14.20	38	82
41	2.57	2	101	3,898	330	59	2314	14.10	39	85
42	2.63	2	101	3,978	328	60	2298	14.00	39	89
43	2.69	2	101	4,057	325	61	2280	13.90	40	92
44	2.74	2	101	4,136	323	62	2262	13.78	41	95
45	**2.80**	2	101	**4,215**	**320**	63	**2243**	**13.67**	42	99
46	**3.30**					63	-63	-0.38	42	129
47	3.44	3	63	2,643	355	62	1546	9.42	42	138
48	3.59	3	63	2,730	355	64	1544	9.41	43	147
49	3.73	3	63	2,816	354	66	1540	9.38	44	157
50	3.88	3	63	2,902	353	68	1532	9.34	46	166
51	4.02	3	63	2,988	351	70	1524	9.28	47	176
52	4.17	3	63	3,073	350	72	1514	9.22	48	187

Figure 33. Simulation

37

The user inputs are shown in the table below:

	K	L	M
1	user inputs		
2	stall	2000	rpm
3	opt	4200	rpm
4	shift	0.50	sec
5	dt1	0.06	sec
6	dt2	0.06	sec
7	dt3	0.14	sec
8	dt4	0.41	sec
9	1/4m	14.08	sec

Figure 34. User Inputs

Here the stall rpm is set to 2000, the shift rpm is set to 4200, the time to shift is set to 0.5 seconds, and the three time steps are 0.06, 0.06, 0.14, and 0.41 seconds for first, second, third, and fourth gears, respectively. The quarter mile time is calculated by interpolation from the distance and time at the bottom of the simulation in fourth gear. In order to satisfy the user inputs, we must adjust the four time steps, and so a macro [solve1] is provided to accomplish this. The code is:

```
Private Sub CommandButton1_Click()
  Dim i As Integer, r1 As Double, r2 As Double, t As
Double
  r1 = Range("L3").Value
  For i = 1 To 10
    r2 = Range("D24").Value
    t = Range("L5").Value
    t = t * (1 + r1 / r2) / 2
    Range("L5").Value = t
  Next i
  For i = 1 To 20
    r2 = Range("D45").Value
    t = Range("L6").Value
    t = t * (1 + r1 / r2) / 2
    Range("L6").Value = t
  Next i
  For i = 1 To 30
    r2 = Range("D66").Value
    t = Range("L7").Value
    t = t * (1 + r1 / r2) / 2
    Range("L7").Value = t
  Next i
  For i = 1 To 40
    r2 = Range("D87").Value
    t = Range("L8").Value
    t = t * (1 + r1 / r2) / 2
    Range("L8").Value = t
  Next i
End Sub
```

38

In order to see the impact on quarter-mile time (i.e., the time required to cover ¼ mile or 1320 feet) we can step through a range of shift rpm and create a table. There is a macro provided for this too [solve2]. That code is:

```
Private Sub CommandButton2_Click()
  Dim rpm As Integer, irow As Integer, iter as integer
  irow = 2
  For rpm = 4000 To 5800 Step 100
    Range("L3").Value = rpm
    for iter= 1 to 3
      Call CommandButton1_Click
    next iter
    irow = irow + 1
    Cells(irow, 15).Value = rpm
    Cells(irow, 16).Value = Range("L9").Value
  Next rpm
End Sub
```

Note that the number of iterations to converge varies and was set to three. The resulting table looks like this:

	N	O	P
1		quarter mile	
2	solve1	shift	sec
3		4000	14.25
4	solve2	4100	14.16
5		4200	14.08
6	solve3	4300	14.01
7		4400	13.93
8		4500	13.86
9		4600	13.79
10		4700	13.73
11		4800	13.67
12		4900	13.61
13		5000	13.55
14		5100	13.50
15		5200	13.45
16		5300	13.41
17		5400	13.37
18		5500	13.33
19		5600	13.31
20		5700	13.28
21		5800	13.26

Figure 35. Buttons and Table

The resulting graph is shown in this next figure:

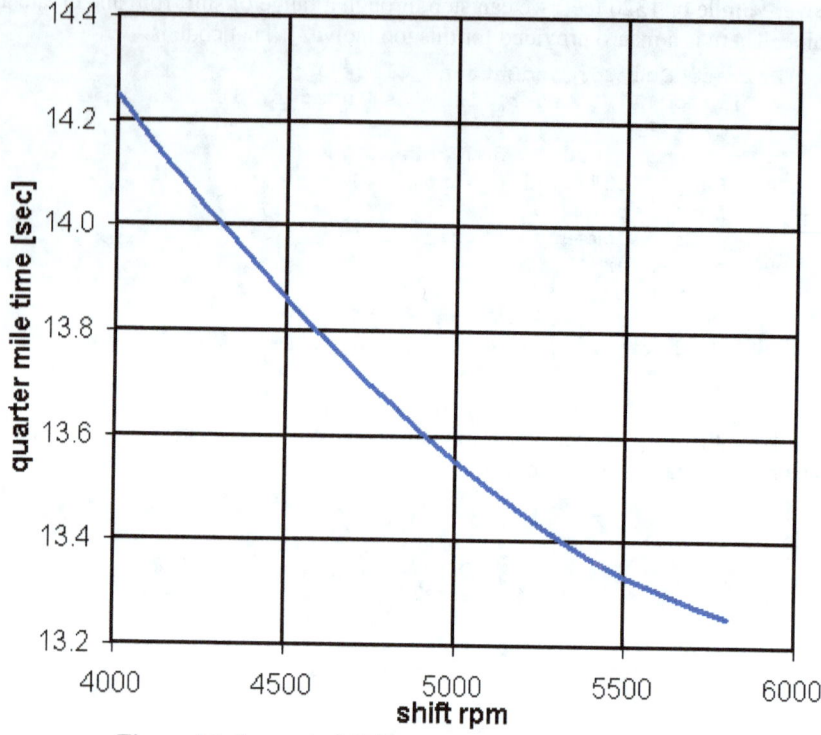

Figure 36. Impact of Shift rpm on Quarter Mile Time

For this particular design (engine, gear ratios, weight, and drag) we don't see an optimum point (i.e., minimum). In this case, the shift rpm is limited by safe engine operation). This is not always the case.

There is one final calculation with this spreadsheet: adjusting the shift rpm so that this is reached as the car crosses the quarter-mile point. There is a third macro [solve3] that adjust the shift ratio until the final position (cell J87) equals 1320 feet. The corresponding solution is 4044 rpm and 14.21 seconds.

In this example we have pulled together several tools and methods, including curve fitting and calculus, in order to solve a dynamic problem involving a machine operation (i.e., a car) in multiple variables. We have also illustrated how to create a user-defined macro to iteratively solve a nonlinear problem (e.g., adjusting each time step to satisfy the shift point). These same methods can be used to solve a wide variety of industrial problems.

Chapter 5. Mechanical Connections

Industrial processes often involve mechanical constraints, which arise from connections such as pulleys and levers. One such problem is shown in this next figure:

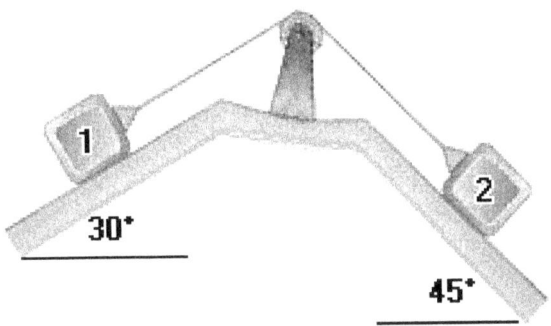

Figure 37. Two Weights and Pulley

If the system is at rest (i.e., the weights are not sliding), what is the tension on the cable?

$$T = w_1 \sin(30°) = w_2 \sin(45°) \qquad (5.1)$$

where T is the tension, w_1 and w_2 are the respective weights, 30° and 45° are the respective angles with respect to the horizontal. If we know either of the weights, we know the other from this equation. If the weights do not satisfy this relationship, the system will move (i.e., one weight will slide up, while the other slides down).

A second example is shown in this next figure:

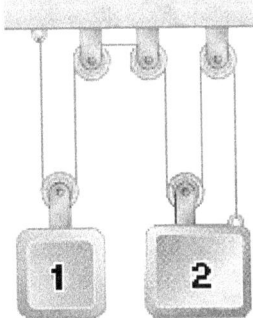

Figure 38. Two Weights and Five Pulleys

41

The tension in the cable is given by:

$$T = \frac{w_1}{2} = \frac{w_2}{3}$$

(5.2)

where T is the tension, w_1 and w_2 are the respective weights. With pulleys (that aren't moving), the tension is equal to the weight divided by the number of links (i.e., 2 and 3 in this case).

Levers

Levers or weights suspended by a bar are similar to the pulleys.

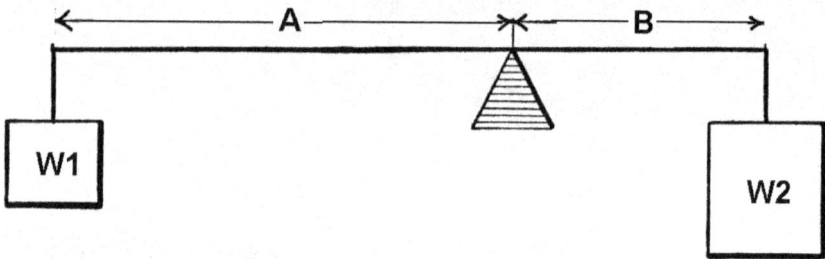

Figure 39. Lever or Suspended Weights

In this case, if the weights are not moving, we see that:

$$Aw_1 = Bw_2$$

(5.3)

We use formulas such as these to build mathematical expressions that represent the processes we seek to optimize.

Chapter 6. Random Events

Some industrial processes may be approximated as random, much like the spin of the roulette wheel or slot machine or lottery. In order to work with such approximations, there are two aspects, which must be considered: 1) the number of possible outcomes and 2) the likelihood of any particular result. We begin with the lottery.

The Pick 5 lottery is based on drawing 5 of 49 balls from a tumbling cylinder. The balls are numbered consecutively 1 through 49; so that there's only one ball with each number. What is the probability of drawing in any order: 1,2,3,4,5? On the first draw any one of 5 out of 49 will work, or 5/49. On the second draw any one of 4 out of 48 will work, or 4/48 and so forth, yielding:

$$\left(\frac{5}{49}\right)\left(\frac{4}{48}\right)\left(\frac{3}{47}\right)\left(\frac{2}{46}\right)\left(\frac{1}{45}\right) = \left(\frac{120}{228,826,080}\right) = \left(\frac{1}{1,906,884}\right) \quad (6.1)$$

The probability of drawing these same five numbers in order is:

$$\left(\frac{1}{49}\right)\left(\frac{1}{48}\right)\left(\frac{1}{47}\right)\left(\frac{1}{46}\right)\left(\frac{1}{45}\right) = \left(\frac{1}{228,826,080}\right) \quad (6.2)$$

The probability of drawing in any order: 3,17,21,25,41 is the same as drawing 1,2,3,4,5 in any order. If the tickets are $1 each and the jackpot is $1,000,000 what is the return?

$$return = \left(\frac{\$1,000,000}{1,906,884}\right) = 52.44\% \quad (6.3)$$

In this case, the winners get 52.44% of the take and the operators of the lottery keep 47.56%, which would be better odd than most. When you consider Churchill Downs it should be obvious that they keep most of the money.

Random Numbers

Occasionally you may need to generate random numbers. Most of the examples in this text are implemented in an Excel™ spreadsheet, which has a built-in random number function, rand(). The in-macro equivalent is Rnd(). Note that this function returns a *uniformly-distributed* random floating-point number between 0 and 1. These have a flat probability distribution (i.e., frequency of occurrence); that is, 0.5 is equally likely as 0.4 or 0.6, which is not likely what you need.

43

If you read articles and papers on simulating random events, most often these discuss *normally-distributed* random numbers; that is, ones whose frequency forms a bell-shaped curve. The respective distribution (i.e., frequency of occurrence) of two types of random numbers are shown in the following figure:

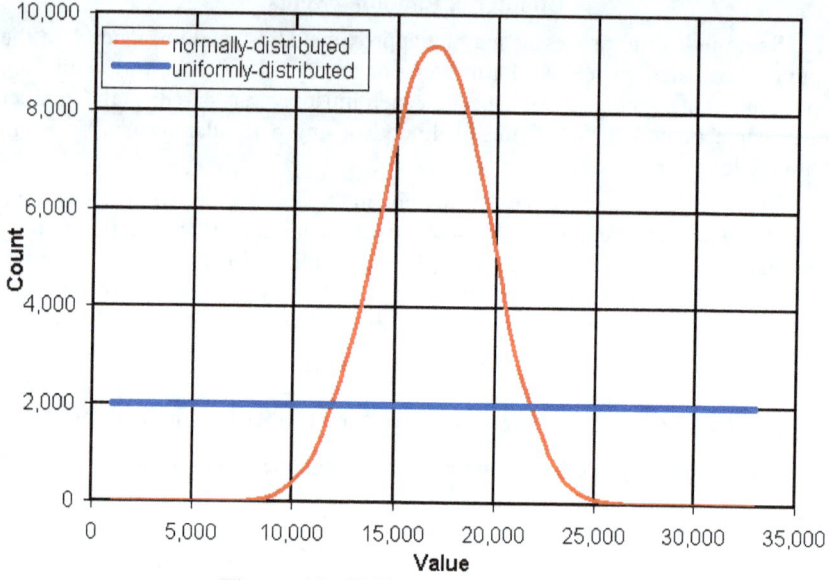

Figure 40. 65,535 Random Integers

The normal distribution is given by:

$$f(\mu, \sigma, x) = \frac{1}{\sqrt{2\pi\sigma^2}} e^{\left[\frac{(x-\mu)^2}{2\sigma^2}\right]} \tag{6.1}$$

where x is the value, μ is the mean, and σ is the standard deviation. Should you need normally-distributed random numbers between -1 and 1 or having an average of a and a standard deviation of s, these two Excel macros will suffice:

```
Function nrand() As Double
   Dim i As Integer
   nrand = -6
   For i = 1 To 12
     nrand = nrand + Rnd()
   Next i
   nrand = nrand / 6
End Function
Function srand(a As Double, s As Double) As Double
   srand = a + s * nrand()
End Function
```

44

We will use these functions in several problems, including traffic simulations.

Clearance

Clearance (i.e., the space between two machined parts) isn't exactly a random process but it is often approximated in this way. We often represent inner and outer diameters and lengths as some average value plus or minus a tolerance. The accuracy of the machines producing such parts is often characterized as normally-distributed random variations. Here we consider a greased sleeve bearing on a typical one horsepower electric motor. The shaft is nominally 5/8" (0.625 inch). In order for this bearing to work properly, the clearance must be 0.001250 ± 0.000625 inch ($1/800^{th} \pm 1/1600^{th}$). The standard deviation of the machining process (boring for the sleeve and turning for the shaft) is 0.000200 inch ($1/5000^{th}$).

We can easily set this problem up as an Excel® spreadsheet (see clearance.xls in the online archive). The first ten rows contain the simulation parameters and labels. The simulation begins on row 11 and continues on to row 65,536. Column A contains the sleeve diameter, column B contains the shaft diameter, and column C contains the clearance. Column D contains a zero or one depending on whether the sleeve/shaft pair must be rejected (i.e., outside the allowable clearance range). There are 1695 rejects (cell D9) or 2.59% of the total, which is disappointing, but acceptable.

	A	B	C	D	E	F	G	H	I	J
1	simulation parameters					0.62400	sleeve	shaft	0.00000	clearance
2	0.626250	0.625000	0.001250	target		0.62405	0	0	0.00005	1
3	0.000200	0.000200	0.000625	tolerance		0.62410	0	0	0.00010	0
4	simulation summary results				allowable	0.62415	0	0	0.00015	0
5	0.627039	0.625803	0.002340	max	0.001875	0.62420	0	0	0.00020	3
6	0.626249	0.625001	0.001248	avg	0.001250	0.62425	0	1	0.00025	6
7	0.625472	0.624246	-0.000011	min	0.000625	0.62430	0	11	0.00030	11
8	0.000199	0.000200	0.000282	stdev		0.62435	0	20	0.00035	28
9		simulation		1695	2.59%	0.62440	0	46	0.00040	38
10	sleeve	shaft	clearance	reject		0.62445	0	90	0.00045	63
11	0.626513	0.624751	0.001762	0		0.62450	0	169	0.00050	103

Figure 41. Spreadsheet to Analyze Shaft Clearance

The maximum clearance is 0.002340 (cell C5), which is highlighted in red with conditional formatting because it's above the maximum (0.001875 cell E5). The minimum clearance is -0.000011 (cell C7) and is also highlighted in red because it's below the minimum (0.000625 cell E7). The sleeve diameter (green curve), shaft diameter (blue curve), and clearance (red curve) all exhibit the familiar bell shape. The sleeve and shaft diameters are inputs to the model and the clearance is simply the difference of the two, so this is not surprising.

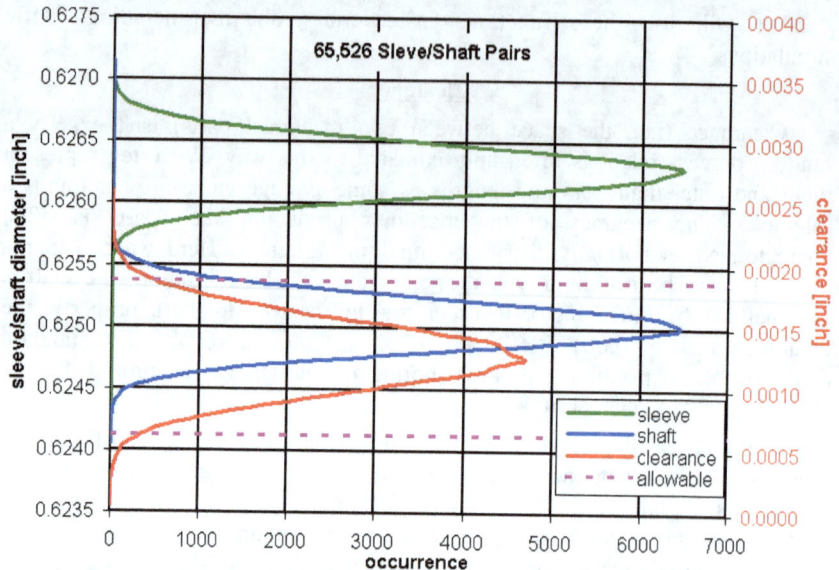

Figure 42. Simulated Frequency of Occurrence

This figure illustrates something you will see elsewhere in this book: a second Y-axis. The clearance is on a considerably different scale than the sleeve and shaft diameters and so must be plotted against a different axis. The sleeve and shaft diameter is plotted on the left Y-axis and the clearance is plotted on the right Y-axis. The label indicates this and so does the color of the numbers. I have intentionally made the numbers and text on the second (i.e., right) Y-axis match the color of the curve that's plotted against that axis (i.e., the red one, clearance). The allowable limits on clearance are also shown (the dashed horizontal magenta lines).

Chapter 7. Word Problems

Practical problems in life and industry are most often posed as word problems. In order to analyze these mathematically, we must develop skills to translate word problems into mathematical expressions. As we illustrate this, we might as well throw in some humor too...

Coyote vs. Roadrunner

ACME Coyote Supply, Inc. is the world's largest manufacturer of roadrunner bait and traps. Coyotes order at least one package of bait with every trap. This relationship can be expressed by the following expression:

$$bait\ orders \geq trap\ orders$$

Less than one-half of the traps are destroyed the first time they're used. Coyotes are likely order more bait for the remaining traps. This relationship can be expressed:

$$bait\ reorders \geq \frac{trap\ orders}{2}$$

No more than one-third of the coyotes who destroy the traps on first use will reorder the same trap. This relationship can be expressed:

$$trap\ reorders \leq \frac{trap\ orders}{3}$$

ACME makes $1.25 off each package of bait and $11.50 off each trap.

$$profit = 1.25 \times bait\ orders + 11.50 \times trap\ reorders$$

If there are 15,000 coyotes in Arizona and it takes 6 weeks to deliver an order, what is ACME's maximum annual sales potential for Arizona?

$$\frac{orders}{year} \leq 15,000 \times \frac{\left(\dfrac{52 weeks}{year}\right)}{\left(\dfrac{6}{order}\right)}$$

The bait works; but the traps don't; because (unbeknownst to the coyotes) ACME is entirely staffed by roadrunners. A roadrunner can build no more than 5 traps a day, which means that:

47

$$roadrunners\ building\ traps \geq \frac{\left(\dfrac{traps\ built}{day}\right)}{\left[\dfrac{\left(\dfrac{5\ traps}{roadrunner}\right)}{day}\right]}$$

A roadrunner can fill 100 zip-lock bags of bait in a day; but ACME must pay one extra roadrunner as foreman to watch the others and make sure they don't eat all the bait. This means that:

$$roadrunners\ bagging\ bait \geq \frac{\left(\dfrac{bags\ of\ bait}{day}\right)}{\left[\dfrac{\left(\dfrac{100}{roadrunner}\right)}{day}\right]} + one\ foreman$$

The Union says if ACME pays a foreman to watch the roadrunners bag bait it must also pay a longshoreman to watch the ones who are building traps, so that...

$$total\ roadrunners \geq roadrunners\ making\ traps$$
$$+\ one\ longshoreman + roadrunners\ bagging\ bait$$
$$+\ one\ foreman$$

Even though coyotes are very optimistic and aren't easily discouraged, they never order more than 5 packages of bait per trap.

$$packages\ of\ bait\ sold \leq \frac{traps\ sold}{5}$$

Rubber Chickens

Cluck, Inc. is the world's largest manufacturer of rubber chickens and accessories. The machinery at the Cluck factory can produce 900,000 rubber chickens per month at peak capacity. Cluck's sales this year are expected to reach 6,750,000. The demand for rubber chickens varies throughout the year. Rubber chickens are a popular stocking stuffer; and Cluck expects to sell 2,500,000 in the week before Christmas alone.

48

Cluck employs a staff of 80 machine operators year round; but these can only operate half the machines. Cluck hires another 80 machine operators for part of the year to make up the difference in production. How many months must the seasonal machine operators work in order to meet the total production?

$$\frac{6,750,000\,chickens}{\left(\dfrac{90,000\,chickens}{full\,capacity\,month}\right)} = 7.5\,full\,capacity\,months$$

$$7.5\,full\,capacity\,months - 6\,full\,time = 1.5months$$

It takes 4 months to get a rubber chicken from Taiwan to the shelves at K-Mart. If the rubber chickens are to arrive before the third week of December for the Christmas buying frenzy, what is the latest in the year that Cluck can hire the seasonal operators?

$$6wks\,manufacturing + 4\,wks\,shipping = 10wks\,lead$$

$$wk\,3December - 10wks\,lead = wk\,2October$$

Rubber chicken accessories include a bright red bandanna, cowboy boots, and a cowboy hat. These must be ordered at the time of original purchase to insure a proper fit. Past sales have shown that one-half the rubber chickens are ordered with a bandanna:

$$bandanas = \frac{chickens}{2}$$

Records show that *Cluck* produces bandannas according to the following relationship:

$$bandanas = chickens - 3,375,000$$

Is this possible? Do these two equations (sales and production) make sense? Combining these two relationships yields:

$$\frac{chickens}{2}?chickens - 3,375,000$$

Substituting the expected number of chickens yields:

$$\frac{6,750,000}{2} = 6,750,000 - 3,375,000$$

So, yes, this works. Past sales have shown that one-third the rubber chickens are ordered with boots:

$$boots = \frac{chickens}{3}$$

Records show that *Cluck* produces boots according to the following relationship:

$$boots = chickens - 4{,}500{,}000$$

Is this possible? Do these two equations (sales and production) make sense? Again, we substitute and compare:

$$\frac{chickens}{3} \; ? \; chickens - 4{,}500{,}000$$

$$\frac{6{,}750{,}000}{3} = 6{,}750{,}000 - 4{,}500{,}000$$

So, yes, this also works. Past sales have shown that one-fourth the rubber chickens are ordered with hats:

$$hats = \frac{chickens}{4}$$

Records show that *Cluck* produces hats according to the following relationship:

$$hats = chickens - 5{,}062{,}500$$

Is this possible? Do these two equations (sales and production) make sense? Again, we substitute and compare:

$$\frac{chickens}{4} \; ? \; chickens - 5{,}062{,}500$$

$$\frac{6{,}750{,}000}{4} = 6{,}750{,}000 - 5{,}062{,}500$$

So, yes, this also works.

Chapter 8. Simple Problems

We now combine these principles in order to consider simple problems. The first example is Apex Television Company, which produces two sizes: 64-inch and 80-inch. They can produce no more than 40 of the smaller units and no more than 10 of the larger ones. The smaller units require 20 hours to assemble and the larger ones require 10 hours. The profit on the smaller units is $120/unit and for the larger ones is $80/unit. We seek the combination that will yield the maximum profit. This problem can be found on the Apex tab of the spreadsheet simple.xls in the online archive.

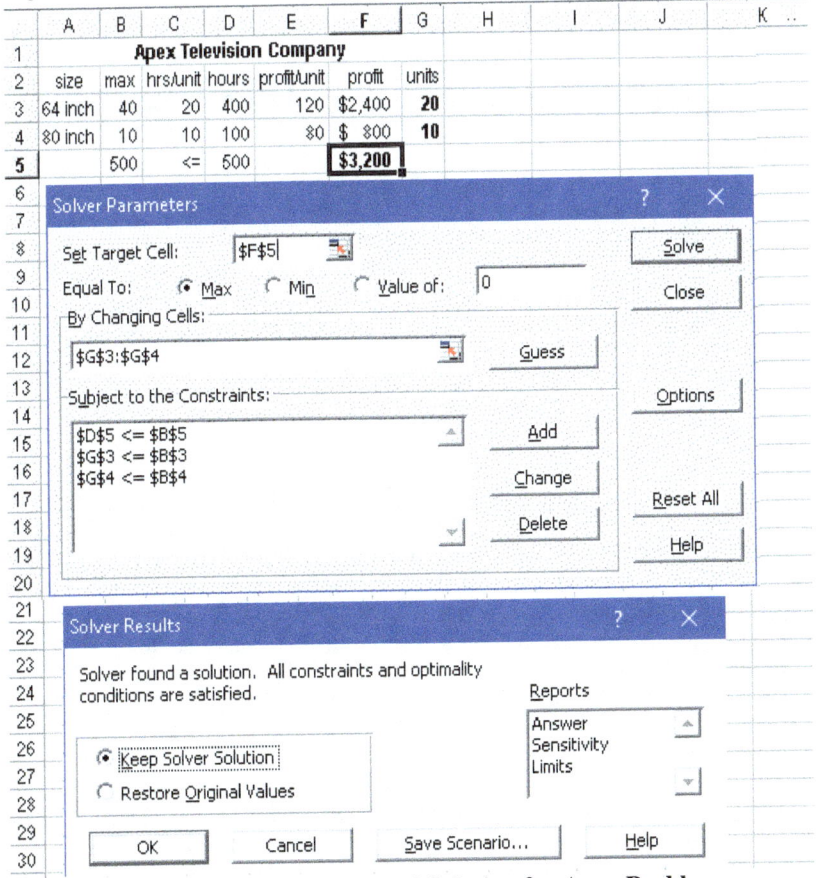

Figure 43. Setup, Solver, and Solution for Apex Problem

Column F is calculated (number of units times profit per unit) and totaled at the bottom, which is the cell we want maximized. The variables, which can be adjusted are in cells G3:G4. The constraints are the maximum units. The Excel Solver finds the optimum solution, which is 20 of the smaller units and 10 of the larger ones with a total profit of $3200.

This next problem is very similar. Window World manufactures two types of windows: wood and aluminum. Each worker can make up to 8 wooden or 8 aluminum windows per hour but only 10 total. The profit on the wood windows is $60 and on the aluminum ones is $30. Find the combination resulting in the maximum profit. This problem can be found on the WW tab of the spreadsheet simple.xls in the online archive.

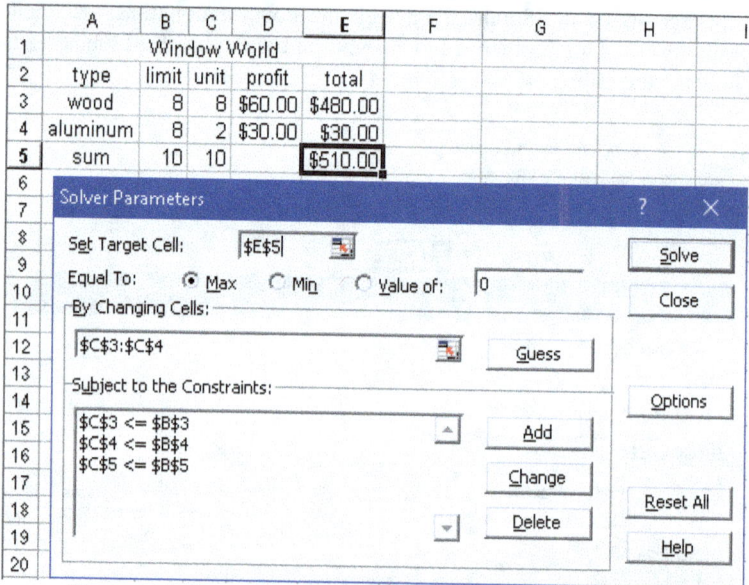

Figure 44. Spreadsheet and Solver for Window Problem

The cell to be maximized is E5 and the variables are C3:C4. The constraints are the limit of each and the total limit. The optimum result is 8 wood plus 2 aluminum. Notice that in both of these examples one of the variables is at the limit while the other one is below. It is often the case that one item or option is maxed out.

Duration/Sequence

One of the more common problems in manufacturing is how long to perform a given process. To illustrate this we consider one line at the Krispy-Kreme doughnut factory, which makes two types of doughnuts: glazed (flat) and crullers (twisted). It takes 15 minutes to clean the machine and an extra 5 minutes to change the head. The machine must be cleaned if the type of batter (glazed/cruller) is changed. The head must be changed if the type of doughnut (glazed/cruller) is changed. The head can only be changed just after the machine is cleaned. The batter must be filled initially and then refilled every 30 minutes. It takes 5 minutes to fill or refill the batter. While the line is operating it makes 4 doughnuts (side-by-side, extruded out into the moving hot oil) every 4 seconds, or 60 per minute. Customers buy 8 times as many glazed doughnuts as crullers. Customers complain if any of the doughnuts are more than 2 hours (120 minutes) old. How often should we clean, refill batter, switch batter, and switch heads so as to create the most doughnuts while meeting all of the constraints? You can find this problem on the KK tab in spreadsheet simple.xls in the online archive. The spreadsheet looks like this:

	A	B	C	D	E	F	G	H	I	J
1	Krispy-Kreme Doughnut Factory									
2	task	time in minutes			doughnuts					
3		duration	begin	end	crullers	glazed	legend			
4	clean	15	0	15			variable			
5	head	5	15	20			linked			
6	fill	5	20	25			constraint			
7	crullers	7	25	32	433		maximized			
8	clean	15	32	47						
9	head	5	47	52						
10	fill	5	52	57						
11	glazed	30	57	87		1800				
12	fill	5	87	92						
13	glazed	28	92	120		1667				
14	clean	15	120	135				120	oldest cruller	
15	head	5	135	140				120	oldest glazed	
16	fill	5	140	145				120	oldest doughnut	
17	crullers	7	145	152	433					
18	clean	15	152	167						
19	head	5	167	172						
20	fill	5	172	177						
21	glazed	30	177	207		1800				
22	fill	5	207	212						
23	glazed	28	212	240		1667				
24	total				867	6933	9467			

Figure 45. Spreadsheet for Doughnut Problem

Column A contains the list of steps in the overall process, which must be performed in a specific order. We begin with two cycles so that the maximum age of the doughnuts between cycles can be calculated. Column B contains the duration of each step. All of these are of fixed duration except for actually making the doughnuts. The cells are color-coded. The yellow cells are the variables we will be adjusting to find the optimum. The orange cells are linked to the yellow ones because the two cycles are the same (by design).

Column C contains the total time or the sum of column B at the beginning of each step and column D contains the end time for each step. Column E contains the number of crullers made and column F contains the number of glazed made. The total of each type are on the bottom line with the total of all highlighted in green, the cell we want to maximize (by changing the two run times, B7 and B13). The age of the oldest doughnut is our constraint, which is calculated from the schedule and highlighted in cyan. The Solver looks like this:

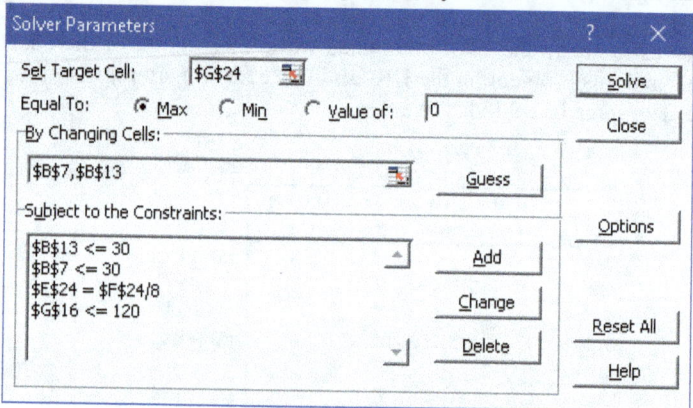

Figure 46. Solver Setup for Doughnut Problem

Here we see the target cell (G24) at the top, (•) Max selected, the variables (B7 and B13), the duration constraints (B7 and B13 ≤ 30 minutes), the desired ratio of cruller to glazed (E14=F24/8), and the age constraint (G16≤120 minutes). The optimum (9467 total doughnuts) is obtained by running crullers for 7.2 minutes and glazed for 27.8 minutes.

Optimal cleaning, changing, and running the peanut butter/cheese cracker lines at the Tom's factory up the road is basically the same problem, only different parameters, expectations, and constraints (i.e., constants). The Tom's cracker factory has two lines that make crackers, one for cheese and the other for peanut butter. One of the lines broke down; so we must make both types of crackers on the remaining line. Customers prefer peanut butter to cheese; so you want to make 3 packages of peanut butter crackers for every 2 packages of cheese crackers.

It takes 4 hours to shut a line off, let it cool down, clean it out, and get it going again making the other type of cracker. Tom's does this once a day even if they're only using it to make one type of cracker, just to satisfy the USDA food safety requirements. Once a line is up and running it can turn out 2 packages of crackers per second or 7200 per hour. Before he died, Old Tom swore that no cracker would be older than 24 hours when it went out the door; and you took an oath to keep that promise. This example may be found on the Toms tab of spreadsheet simple.xls in the online archive. The problem looks like this:

54

	A	B	C	D	E	F
1			Tom's Crackers			
2	cycle		hours		units	
3		begin	run	end	peanut	cheese
4	clean	0.0	4.0	4.0		
5	peanut	4.0	9.6	13.6	69,120	
6	clean	13.6	4.0	17.6		
7	cheese	17.6	6.4	24.0		46,080
8	clean	24.0	4.0	28.0		
9	peanut	28.0	9.6	37.6	69,120	
10	clean	37.6	4.0	41.6		
11	cheese	41.6	6.4	48.0		46,080
12	repeat				total	115,200

Figure 47. Tom's Cracker Problem

Columns B, C, and D contain the beginning, run, and end (completion) time of each sequence in hours. The two variables are in cells C5 and C7 for the peanut butter and cheese runs, respectively. The crackers produced appear in columns E and F with the total in cell F12, which is maximized. The constraint is shown in cyan (cells E5 and F7), which must satisfy the desired ratio of peanut butter to cheese crackers (3 to 2). The Solver looks like this:

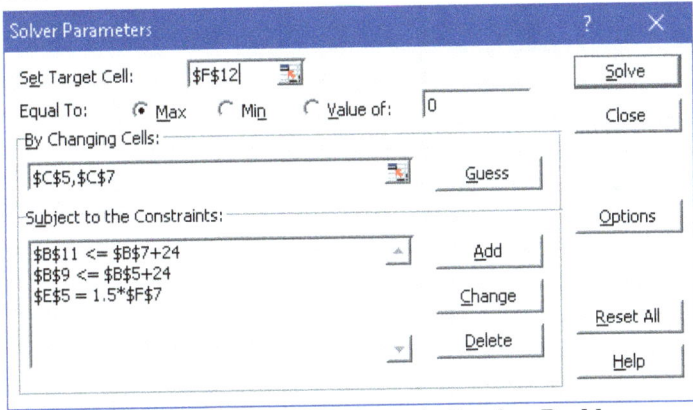

Figure 48. Solver Setup for Tom's Cracker Problem

The target is at the top (F12, the total number of crackers). The (•) Max option is selected. The cells to adjust (i.e., variables) are C5 and C7. The constraints are the age of the crackers (B9 and B11) no more than 24 hours and the ratio (E5=1.5*F7). The solution is to run peanut butter for 9.6 hours and cheese for 6.4 hours, which yields 115,200 crackers total, while satisfying all of the requirements.

The Tom's factory actually has two separate lines, an older one and a newer one. These may not be the same and so we next consider an example involving a choice between production lines...

The Wacky Widget factory makes plastic things to put in Happy Meals. Wacky Widget has two assembly lines: one old and one new. The old assembly line can be up and running in just 2 days, spewing out 2000 widgets per day. The new assembly line is more complicated to set up, taking 7 days; plus it takes several days more to reach peak capacity; but when it's up and running it can spew out 4000 widgets per day. This behavior is shown in the following figure:

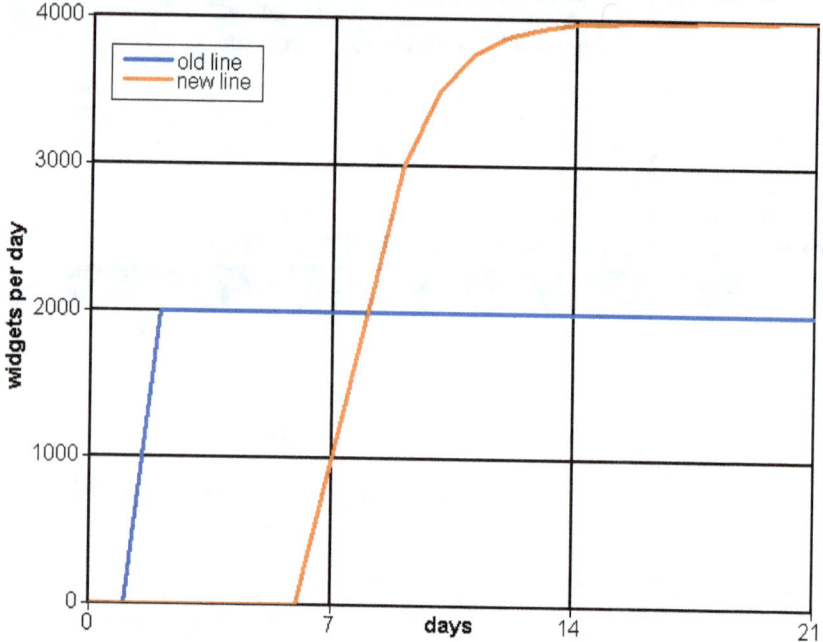

Figure 49. Old and New Widget Production Line Curves

Here we see that the new line overtakes the old (the curves cross) after 8 days. If you have an order for 2000 widgets and schedule is not a problem, you would probably select the old line to accomplish this. If you have an order for 2000 widgets and the customer wants them ASAP, you would definitely choose the old line.

The cumulative total widgets produced over a month (30 days) on the two respective lines is shown in this next curve:

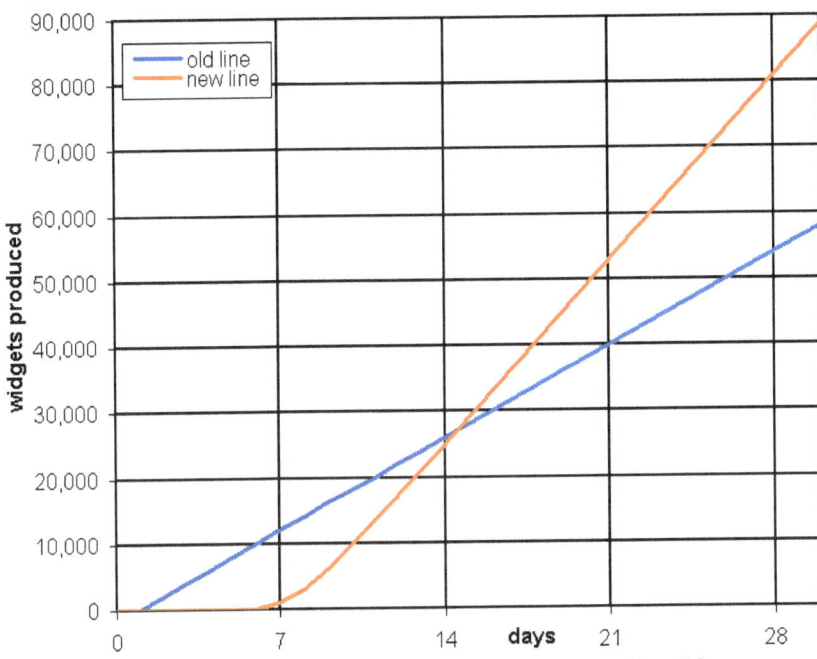

Figure 50. Cumulative Widgets Produced by the Two Lines

Here we see that the cumulative total widgets produced by the new line overtakes the old line (the curves cross) at 15 days. If you had an order for 50,000 widgets, the old line could produce these in 26 days while the new line could produce these in just 20 days. And so we see that the choice of which line to use depends on how many widgets are required and how soon they must be delivered. If these same lines are used to produce other products, the choice becomes more complicated. Still, being able to express the problem mathematically can help make the best (i.e., optimal) decision.

Another way of looking at this same information, which is easily displayed in an Excel spreadsheet is the number of days required to produce a given number of widgets using each line (old or new):

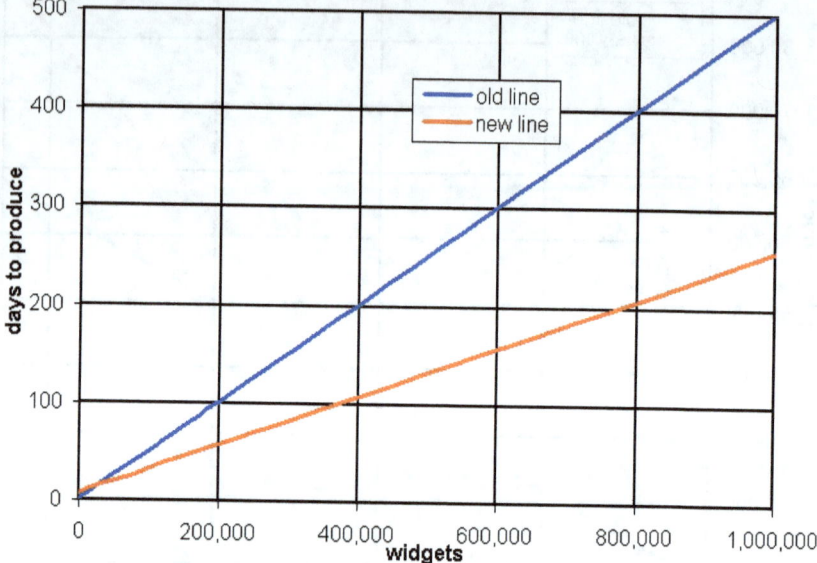

Figure 51. Time Required to Produce Widgets

Chapter 9. Curve-Fitting

Sometimes when formulating mathematical expressions for logistical problems, curve-fitting is necessary. Excel can be quite useful in this, able to provide nonlinear and even multivariate regressions. These next few examples illustrate how this can be accomplished. The first problem is linear. We must make 50,000 Tickle-Me-Elmo before December 1st. We have historical data for the manufacturing process shown in this table:

production		
days	units	units/day
138	29,146	211
51	9,710	190
85	21,022	247
191	37,790	198
231	46,918	203
30	7,708	257
328	69,548	212
300	63,311	211
209	41,905	201
76	12,002	158
18	2,444	136
24	5,503	229
335	74,403	222
37	7,766	210
253	57,976	229
295	63,654	216
358	81,050	226
94	20,085	214
272	65,517	241
263	63,271	241
160	37,901	237
221	49,839	226
223	49,550	222
81	21,881	270
etc...	etc...	etc...

The data along with a linear trend are shown in this next figure:

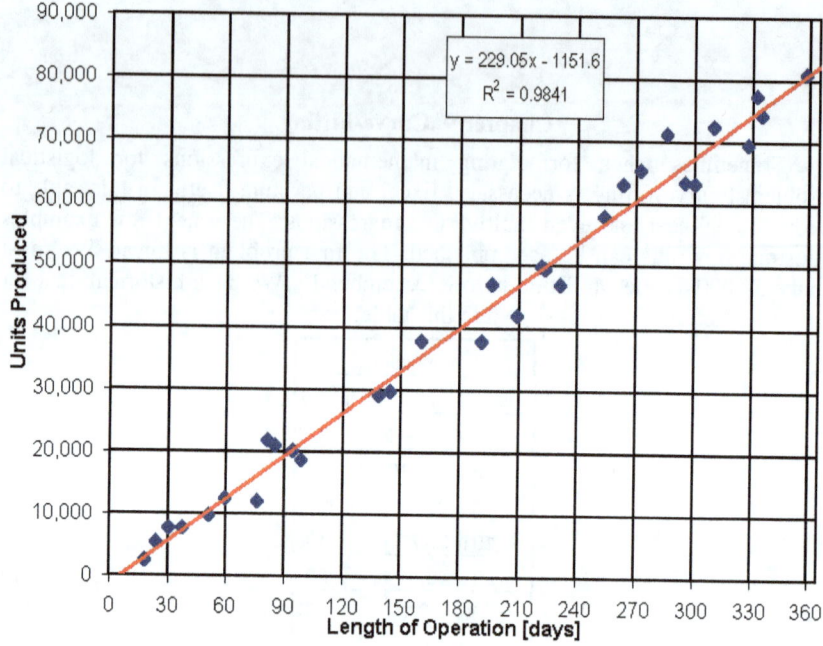

Figure 52. Tickle-Me-Elmo Production History

The equation of a line is $y=a*x+b$. You can obtain the coefficients using the Excel functions a=slope()=229 and b=intercept()=-1152. The goodness of fit is also shown in the figure (R^2=98.36%), which is certainly adequate. These data indicate that it will take approximately:

$$x = \frac{y-b}{a} = \frac{50000-(-1152)}{229} = 223\,days \qquad (9.1)$$

December 1 is day 335 (336 on leap years). The latest to start production would be 223 days before this or April 22. This example may be found on the Elmo tab in spreadsheet curve_fitting.xls in the online archive.

Higher Order Curves

We next reconsider the data behind the widget example in the previous chapter. The rate of production does begin at zero and increase over time, but it's not exactly a smooth transition from stop to full output. Still, in order to effectively model and manage it, we have expectations about what the relationship between run time and production should be.

60

The data collected from past operation is shown in the following table:

production			
$y=ax^2/(1+bx+cx^2)$			
min	u/m	fit	err
77	784	617	-167
143	877	927	50
11	10	16	6
109	802	827	25
197	976	973	-3
131	786	901	115
259	1049	974	-75
185	997	968	-29
95	878	753	-125
35	191	174	-17
113	889	844	-45
167	932	957	25
245	1016	976	-40
67	286	521	235
137	999	915	-84
101	747	788	41
53	423	368	-55
181	984	966	-18
253	1038	975	-63
235	914	976	62
209	904	975	71
23	89	75	-14
etc.	etc.	etc.	etc.

We want the curve to begin at zero, rise gradually (i.e., not linearly), and level off at a maximum. The simplest formula exhibiting this behavior is $y=ax^2/(1+bx+cx^2)$, which is shown at the top of the table. As we move forward in time ($x\to\infty$) the value approaches a constant ($y\to a/c$). Initially, this function increases like x^2. We use the Excel Solver to find the coefficients which best fit the data. To do this, we assign three cells (F2:F5) to contain a,b,c and pick some initial values (in this case most anything will do). We add a column which contains the value calculated using the formula (Column C, labeled 'fit') and another column containing the error between the data and fit (Column D, labeled 'err'). At the bottom we sum the square of the errors using the Excel function =SUMSQ(D4:D47). We use the Solver to adjust a,b,c in order to obtain the lest square error as shown here:

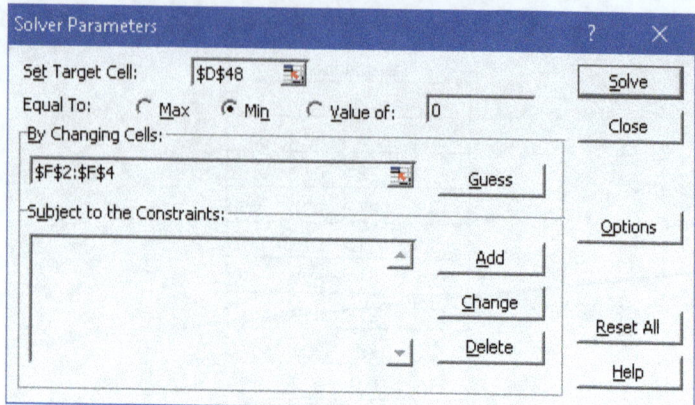

Figure 53. Solver Setup for Problem

The cell to be minimized (sum-square-error) is D48. The cells to adjust (a,b,c) are F2:F4. The minimum is desired this time (before we have sought the maximum). The result is a=0.1239, b=-0.008714, c=0.0001457. The resulting curve is shown in this next figure:

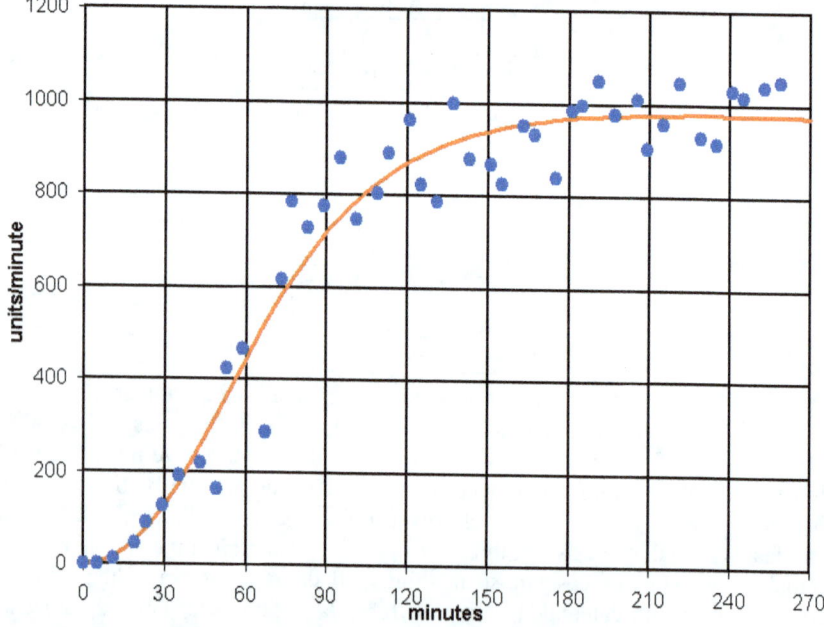

Figure 54. Targeted Curve-Fit through Data

We can now use the coefficients and curve fit to solve production problems. This example may be found on the ramp tab of spreadsheet curve_fitting.xls in the online archive.

Multivariate Problems

We next consider a problem involving three variables, two independent and one dependent, which we will refer to as x,y,z. This same data was used to create the last figure in Chapter 3. The data are shown below as a labeled scatter plot:

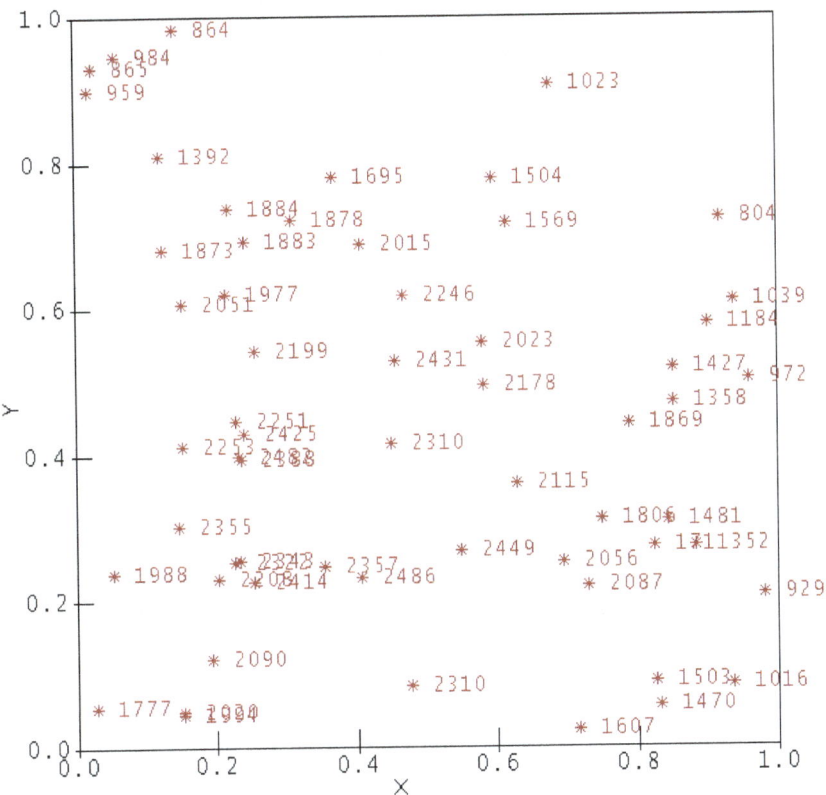

Figure 55. Labeled Scatter Plot

TP2 is one of very few programs that will label a scatter plot with the value of the points.

Tecplot™ will color the dots based on the z value, as shown in this next figure:

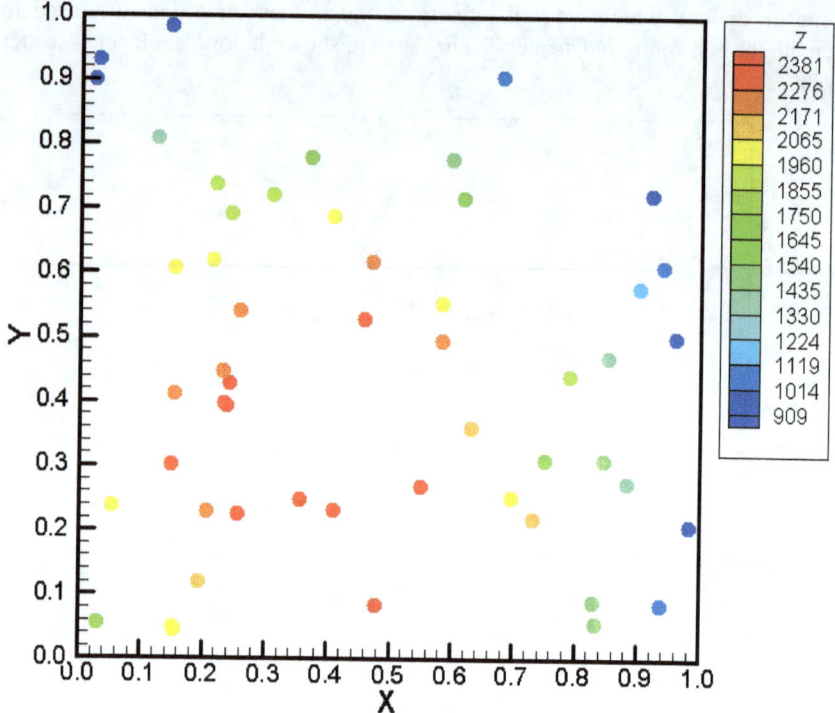

Figure 56. Points Colored Based on Value

In order to use this data in a process model, we must obtain an approximation. Perhaps the simplest one would be:

$$z(x,y)=a+bx+cy+dx^2+exy+fy^2$$

There are many tools available for obtaining such. One example is Curvefit, which is free at the link below the Preface. The data can be found on the scatter tab of spreadsheet curve_fitting.xls in the online archive. One need only copy the data from the Excel spreadsheet and paste it into the Curvefit window, as shown here:

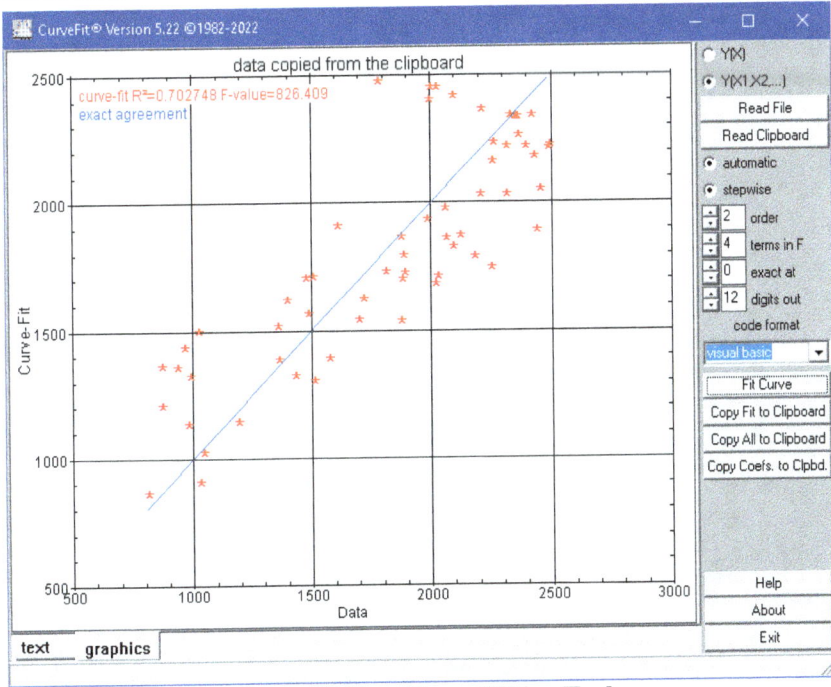

Figure 57. Free Curve-Fitting Tool

Curvefit will not only perform the regression but will also create an Excel macro and put it on the clipboard ready to be pasted into the spreadsheet (press alt-F11 to open macros).

```
curve_fitting.xls - Module1 (Code)
(General)                                        Y

    Option Explicit
    Function Y(X1 As Double, X2 As Double) As Double
      Y = 1570.53280277
      Y = Y + 2862.84699715 * X1
      Y = Y + 2122.89339039 * X2
      Y = Y - 3810.67289986 * X1 ^ 2
      Y = Y - 122.831814668 * X1 * X2
      Y = Y - 3199.72679732 * X2 ^ 2
    End Function
```

Figure 58. Curve-Fit Pasted into Excel from Curvefit

You can get these same coefficients from Excel using the following:

```
=LINEST(C3:C62,Y3:AC62,TRUE,TRUE)
```

You must first set up the columns for x, y, x^2, xy, and y^2 together in a single block, as illustrated below:

Y	Z	AA	AB	AC
		linest setup		
x	y	x^2	xy	y^2
0.124	0.808	0.015	0.100	0.653
0.242	0.428	0.059	0.104	0.183
0.409	0.232	0.167	0.095	0.054
0.939	0.611	0.882	0.574	0.373
0.853	0.471	0.728	0.402	0.222
0.155	0.045	0.024	0.007	0.002
0.697	0.253	0.486	0.176	0.064
0.920	0.724	0.846	0.666	0.524
0.550	0.269	0.303	0.148	0.072

Figure 59. Block for Using Excel's LINEST Function

The results are shown below along with the function with the coefficients highlighted in different colors:

AD	AE	AF	AG	AH	AI
-3199.73	-122.832	-3810.67	2122.893	2862.847	1570.533
176.8418	144.1014	166.8472	194.8991	188.545	53.91411
0.975764	82.74232	#N/A	#N/A	#N/A	#N/A
434.816	54	#N/A	#N/A	#N/A	#N/A
14884388	369699.8	#N/A	#N/A	#N/A	#N/A

Function Y(X1 As Double, X2 As Double) As Double
Y = 1570.53280277
Y = Y + 2862.84699715 * X1
Y = Y + 2122.89339039 * X2
Y = Y - 3810.67289986 * X1 ^ 2
Y = Y - 122.831814668 * X1 * X2
Y = Y - 3199.72679732 * X2 ^ 2
End Function

Figure 60. LINEST Function Results

Note that the coefficients are the same but not in the same order. More information about the **LINEST** function is available with the built-in help feature. The additional information (below the row of highlighted numbers) provides a statistical analysis for the process, including the sum-square-error and the correlation coefficient, R^2, which in this case is 0.975764.

Having applied the regression and obtained a function approximating the data, we can now use this along with the other features of Excel to find the optimal operating point.

Chapter 10. Log-Normal Events

We will next consider parameters that can be characterized by a log-normal distribution, that is, ones whose (natural) log exhibits a bell-shaped frequency distribution. While the previous parameters might take on any value (including positive, negative, and zero), log-normal parameters cannot. These never quite reach zero, can get quite large, and can't possibly be negative. Examples include: reaction/response times, time required for different people to accomplish a given task, and time to spread infectious diseases.

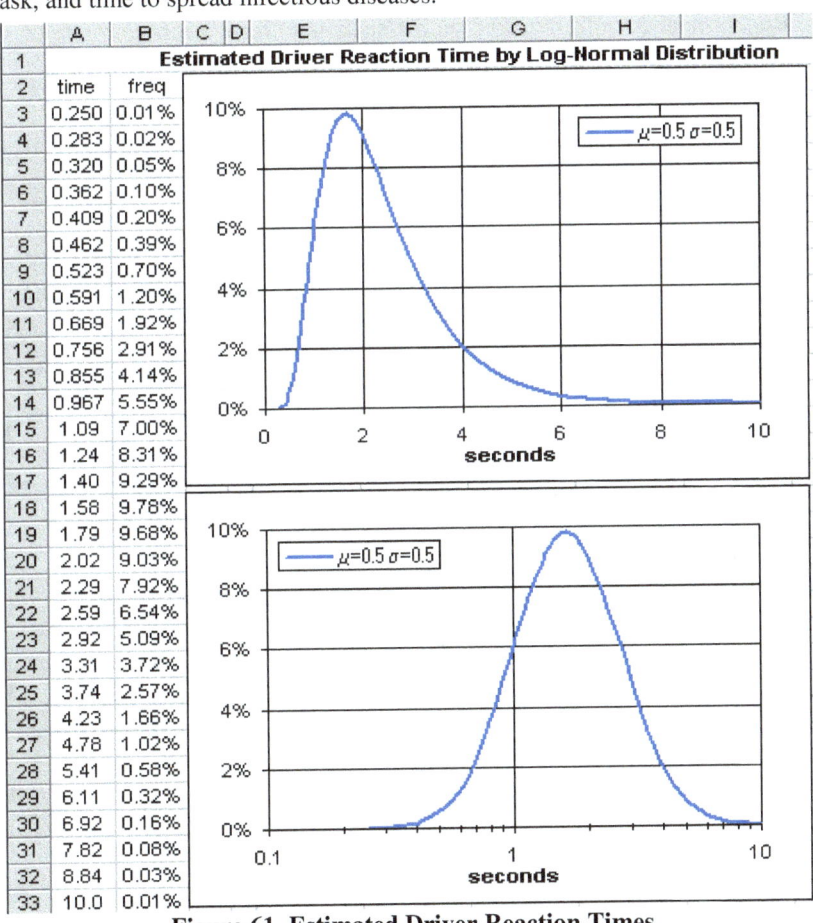

Figure 61. Estimated Driver Reaction Times

The bottom curve has the familiar bell-shape but the horizontal axis is logarithmic. The top curve has the log-normal shape. We see things that exhibit this behavior, at least statistically. For example, drivers who are aware of their surroundings are often fascinated (and/or irritated) with the wide disparity in human reaction rates, especially in traffic. Reaction rates of some drivers can be astonishingly long, depending on how many people they are texting as they wait for the light to change. It just seems like these are most often the first car in line so that they make it through but no one behind them does.

The reaction rate of drivers can be roughly estimated by a log-normal distribution having both a mean ($\mu=0.5$ sec) and standard deviation ($\sigma=0.5$ sec) of one-half second, as illustrated in the previous figure. On row 3 we see that 1% of drivers (one out of a hundred on the fast side) have a reaction rate of 0.25 (1/4th) of a second. On the other end of the spectrum, on row 33 we see that 1% of drivers (one out of a hundred on the slow side) have a reaction time of 10 seconds. We replace x by $ln(x)$ in Equation 6.1 to get the log-normal:

$$f(\mu, \sigma, x) = \frac{1}{\sqrt{2\pi\sigma^2}} e^{\left[\frac{(\ln(x)-\mu)^2}{2\sigma^2}\right]} \tag{10.1}$$

This formula is built into Excel and is easily accessed:

`=NORMDIST(LN(x),mu,sigma,FALSE)`

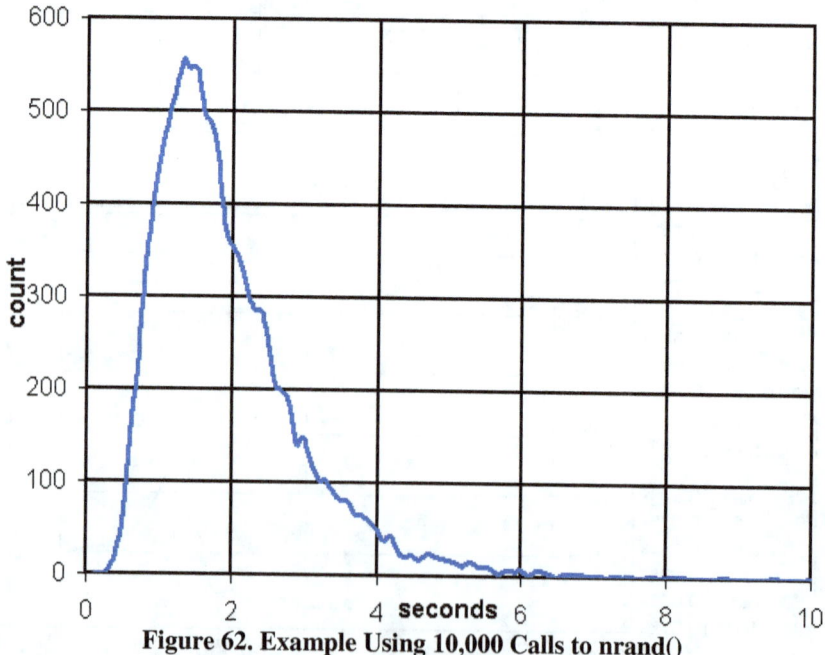

Figure 62. Example Using 10,000 Calls to nrand()

The preceding figure shows that the nrand() Excel macro listed just below Equation 6.1 does yield the correct values. The details can be found on the nrand tab of the spreadsheet driver.xls in the online archive. Another useful macro provided in this same spreadsheet counts the number of values in a list that are greater than or equal to some minimum ($x \geq a$) and less than or equal to some maximum ($x \leq b$):

$$=CountBetween(list,a,b)$$

This function is used to count the number of random numbers between each interval from low to high and thus generate the curve as shown.

Simplest Traffic Example

We can use this calculation ($=exp(nrand())$) as illustrated on the sim1 tab of this spreadsheet to create the simplest traffic simulation in which cars are counted as passing through the intersection as long as the accumulated reaction time is less than or equal to the duration of the green. This looks like:

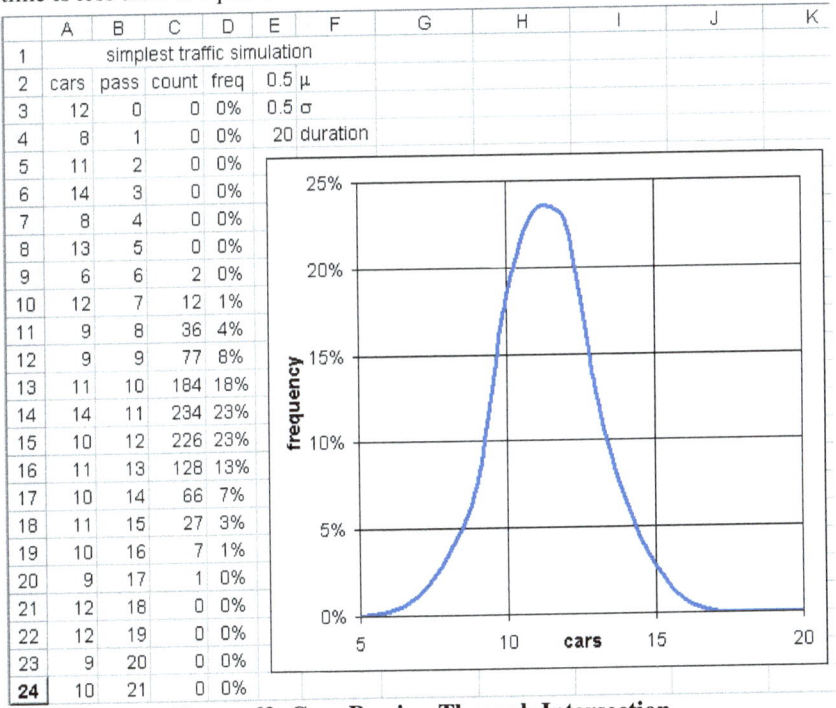

	A	B	C	D	E	F
1		simplest traffic simulation				
2	cars	pass	count	freq	0.5	μ
3	12	0	0	0%	0.5	σ
4	8	1	0	0%	20	duration
5	11	2	0	0%		
6	14	3	0	0%		
7	8	4	0	0%		
8	13	5	0	0%		
9	6	6	2	0%		
10	12	7	12	1%		
11	9	8	36	4%		
12	9	9	77	8%		
13	11	10	184	18%		
14	14	11	234	23%		
15	10	12	226	23%		
16	11	13	128	13%		
17	10	14	66	7%		
18	11	15	27	3%		
19	10	16	7	1%		
20	9	17	1	0%		
21	12	18	0	0%		
22	12	19	0	0%		
23	9	20	0	0%		
24	10	21	0	0%		

Figure 63. Cars Passing Through Intersection

Column A (cars) lists each of the random simulations, as measured by cars passing through. Column B is just the sequence 1 to 24 cars. Column C is the =CountBetween() 1 and 2, 2 and 3, 3 and 4, and so on. Column D is the count (Column C) normalized as a percentage of the total. There are 1000 "simulations" (A3:A1002). Not surprisingly, the overall result (blue curve)

69

exhibits a bell-shape with a mean of about 11.3 and a standard deviation of about 1.64. The Excel macro which calculates the number of cars is:

```
Function cars_pass(mean As Double, stdev As Double,
        duration As Double) As Integer
  Dim r As Double, s As Double, green As Boolean
  cars_pass = 0
  s = 0
  green = True
  While (green)
    r = Exp(ndist(mean, stdev))
    s = s + r
    If (s <= duration) Then
      cars_pass = cars_pass + 1
    Else
      green = False
    End If
  Wend
End Function
```

which adds cars with drivers having a random (log-normal) reaction time until the light changes. While this example uses cars and drivers, it could just as easily be applied to workers making widgets or sorting packages or filling orders from shelved items, putting these in an appropriate-sized box, printing a label, and plopping them on a conveyor belt. Because traffic is so much a part of every-day life we will consider a few more such examples before moving on to widgets and packages.

Note that the mean in this example is a user input (cell E2) and so is the standard deviation (cell E3) and the duration (cell E4). One reason for building such models in an Excel spreadsheet is that we can readily change the parameters and see what happens. We can even use this process (trial-and-error) to pick which parameters best fit a particular industrial process by changing each until the model best approximates observations.

We first change the duration of green to 15, 20, 25 seconds. The result is shown in this next figure:

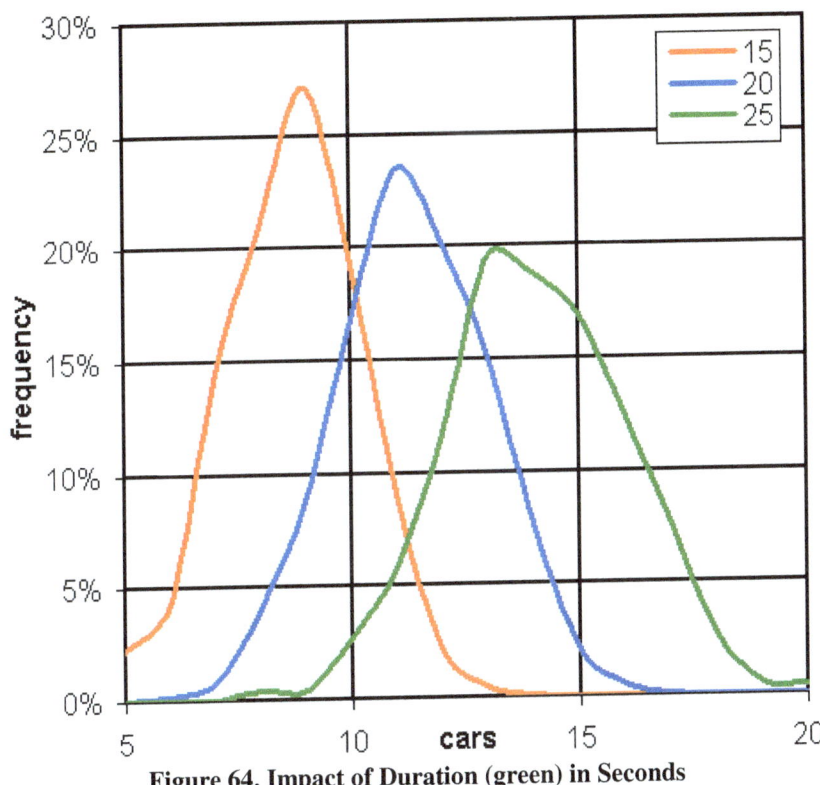

Figure 64. Impact of Duration (green) in Seconds

Reducing the duration to 15 seconds (-25% time) decreases the mean (average number of cats getting through one light change) to about 8½ (-25% cars). Expanding the duration to 25 seconds (+25% time) increases the mean to about 13 (+15% cars). Here we see a disproportionate change; that is, a diminishing return. This is significant, not only for traffic but also for industrial processes. Merely increasing or decreasing one thing or other does not necessarily result in a proportionate change in the outcome. Not only would doubling the typical duration of traffic lights produce much frustration, it would not necessarily move more traffic.

We might be able to improve the mean reaction time of drivers if cars had a feature to disable iPhones whenever the engine is running. We might also improve worker (or student) times by collecting their iPhones at the door. This is shown in the following figure:

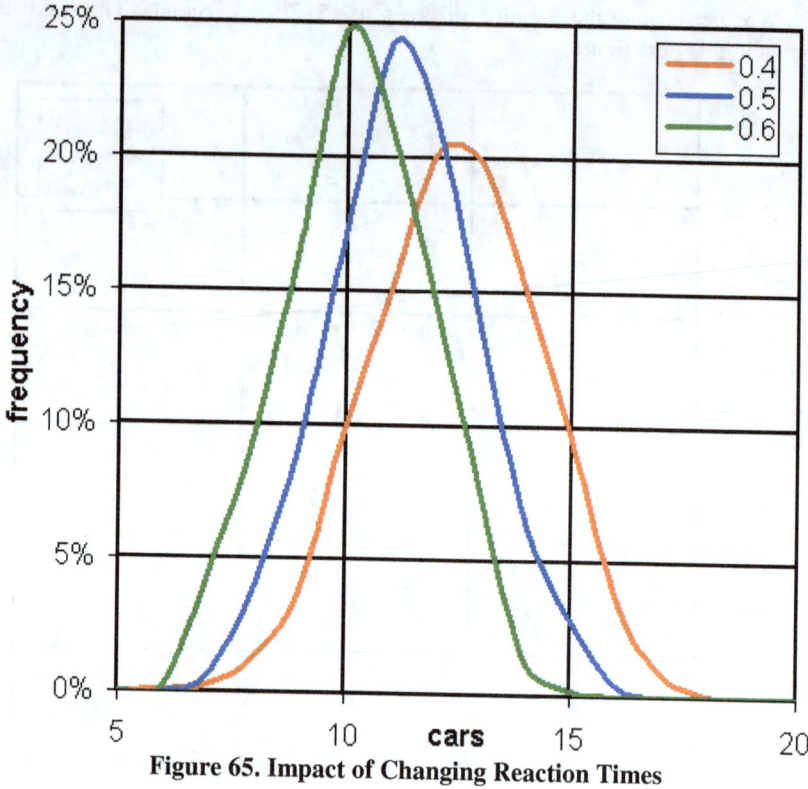

Figure 65. Impact of Changing Reaction Times

We see that the peaks (mean number of cars passing) shifts with changes in the reaction time, as does the width (spread). In each case, the area under the curve is equal to the total number of cars making it through the green.

If we change the standard deviation we see the following change:

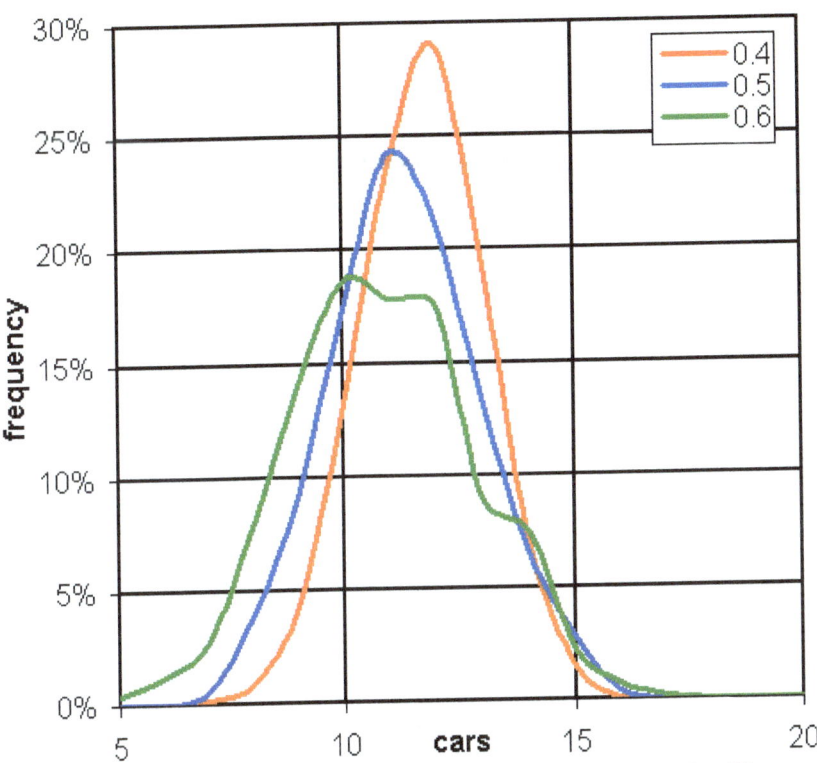

Figure 66. Impact of Changing Standard Deviation of Reaction Time

The distorted shape (lumpiness) of the green curve ($\sigma=0.6$) in this case is due to the limited number of cases (1000). If we increased this number to 10,000 the curve would have the bell shape.

Adding Details

In order to model practical industrial examples, we must consider more details. We now have the tools to develop a more realistic traffic simulation, which is the next step. The number of cars making it through the green has been calculated based purely on driver reaction times estimated by a log-normal distribution. The rate of traffic arrival is definitely biased. We expect a large surge in the morning and another large surge in the evening due to work schedules with a smaller surge mid-day. We can approximate this by:

```
cars=r₁*NORMDIST(t,μ₁,σ₁,FALSE)
     +r₂*NORMDIST(t,μ₂,σ₂,FALSE)
     +r₃*NORMDIST(t,μ₃,σ₃,FALSE)
```

73

where r_1, r_2, r_3 are the three respective rates (cars/minute) of the three surges (morning, noon, and evening), numerically equal to 25, 100, and 25, respectively. The mean times (μ_1, μ_2, μ_3) are 7:30 AM, 12:30 PM, and 5:30 PM, respectively. The three standard deviations (σ_1, σ_2, σ_3) are 0.02, 0.20, and 0.02 days, respectively. [Note: These seem like small numbers but realize that Excel saves dates as floating-point numbers, counting the days since 1/1/1900 so that one hour $=1/24$ and one minute $=1/24/60$.] The user inputs are shown below:

	A	B	C	D	E	F
1	Simulated Car Arrival Rate					
2	12:30 AM	9	0	mean	rate	stdev
3	1:30 AM	14	12	7:30 AM	25	0.02
4	2:30 AM	23	30	12:30 PM	100	0.20
5	3:30 AM	34	59	5:30 PM	25	0.02
6	4:30 AM	50	101			
7	5:30 AM	69	160	cars		
8	6:30 AM	148	269			
9	7:30 AM	615	650	driver reaction rate		
10	8:30 AM	198	1057	0.5 μ		sec
11	9:30 AM	164	1238	0.5 σ		sec
12	10:30 AM	183	1411	20 duration		
13	11:30 AM	195	1600	light durations		
14	12:30 PM	199	1797	green	17	sec
15	1:30 PM	195	1995	yellow	3	sec

Figure 67. User Inputs for Traffic Example

The traffic arrival inputs are highlighted in yellow. The driver reaction inputs are highlighted in green. The traffic light durations are highlighted in cyan. Here we are combining three processes (car arrivals, driver reactions, and light durations) as independent normally-distributed variables. The simulation code (macro) that brings it all together is activated by pushing the [cars] button.

```
Option Explicit
Private Sub CommandButton1_Click()
    Application.Calculation = xlCalculationManual
    Application.ScreenUpdating = False
    Dim i As Integer, r As Double, t As Double, r1 As
        Double, r2 As Double, n As Integer
    Dim t1 As Double, t2 As Double, t3 As Double, t0 As
        Double, r3 As Double
    Dim s1 As Double, s2 As Double, s3 As Double, mu As
        Double, sigma As Double
    t0 = Range("A2").Value
    t1 = Range("D3").Value
    t2 = Range("D4").Value
    t3 = Range("D5").Value
    r1 = Range("E3").Value
    r2 = Range("E4").Value
    r3 = Range("E5").Value
    s1 = Range("F3").Value
    s2 = Range("F4").Value
```

74

```
    s3 = Range("F5").Value
    mu = Range("D10").Value
    sigma = Range("D11").Value
    n = Range("C25").Value
    i = 0
    While (i < n)
      r = Rnd()
      If (r <= r1 / (r1 + r2 + r3)) Then
        t = ndist(t1, s1)
      ElseIf (r <= (r1 + r2) / (r1 + r2 + r3)) Then
        t = ndist(t2, s2)
      Else
        t = ndist(t3, s3)
      End If
      If (t >= t0 And t < t0 + 1) Then
        i = i + 1
        Cells(i + 1, 7).Value = t
        Cells(i + 1, 8).Value = Exp(ndist(mu, sigma))
      End If
    Wend
    Range("G2:H2").Select
    Range(Selection, Selection.End(xlDown)).Select
    Selection.Sort Key1:=Range("G2"), Order1:=xlAscending,
      Header:=xlNo, _
      OrderCustom:=1, MatchCase:=False,
        Orientation:=xlTopToBottom
    Application.Calculation = xlCalculationAutomatic
    Application.ScreenUpdating = True
End Sub
```

We first turn off automatic calculations with:

```
Application.Calculation = xlCalculationManual
```

and turn off screen updating with:

```
Application.ScreenUpdating = False
```

If we don't do these two things, it will take a very long time to process. We turn these both back on after the calculations are over. We next gather the user inputs from the spreadsheet in the respective cells. [Don't move these or the macro will fail.] We then step through the simulation until the time runs out (i.e., from midnight to midnight).

The three hump (big, small, big / morning, noon, evening) expected load pattern (number of cars arriving per hour per lane, which could be some industrial demand) is shown in this next figure:

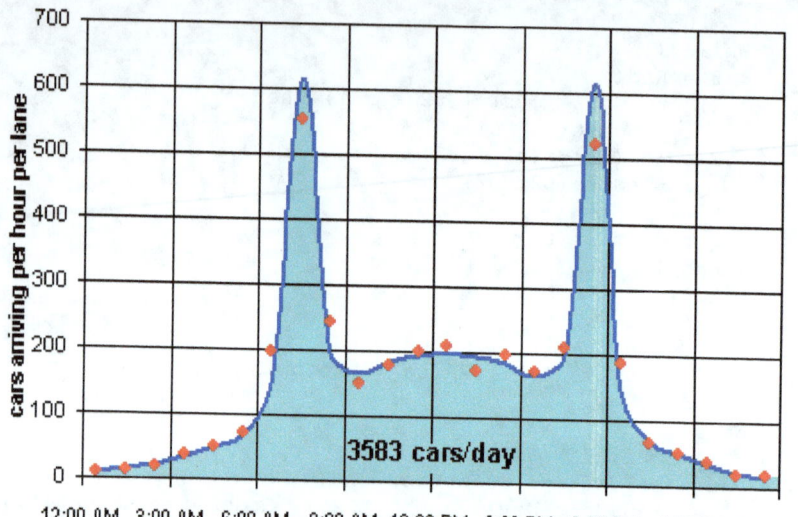

Figure 68. Expected Load (Car Arrival Rate)

The cumulative number of cars (which could be packages that must be sorted and delivered or widgets made) is shown in this next figure:

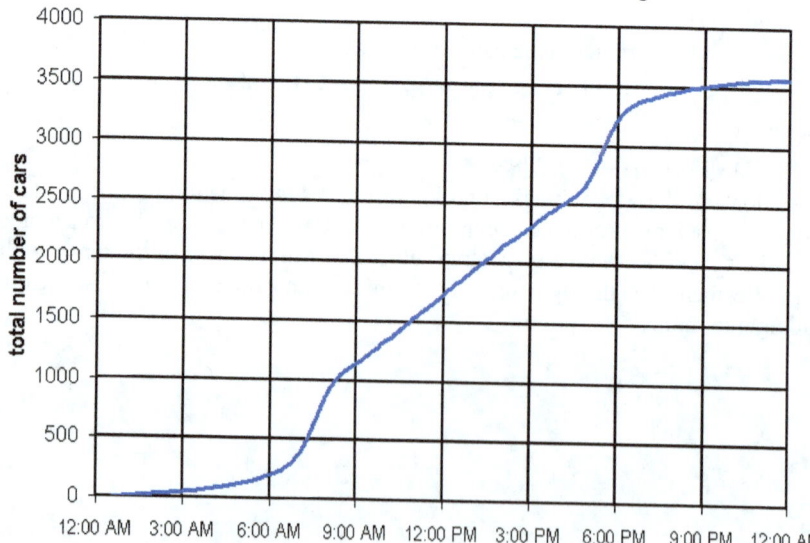

Figure 69. Cumulative Number of Cars

The simulation itself is quite long. The top (beginning/early times) of the results are shown below [There is one row for each car.]:

G	H	I	J	K	L	M	N	O
arrival	reaction	cars	rate	reaction	freq	cars	cycle	envelope
12:32:47 AM	2.59	1	7	0.38		0	49	0
12:33:03 AM	0.60	2	23	0.44	5	0	49	0
12:33:43 AM	0.74	3	18	0.49	17	0	50	0
12:51:49 AM	1.60	4	34	0.56	23	0	77	0
12:52:53 AM	1.48	5	45	0.63	43	0	79	0
12:55:43 AM	3.50	6	75	0.72	67	0	83	0
12:58:09 AM	2.88	7	174	0.81	100	0	87	0
1:04:00 AM	0.81	8	521	0.92	162	0	95	0
1:08:17 AM	0.71	9	247	1.04	206	0	102	0
1:09:13 AM	0.84	10	193	1.18	284	0	103	0
1:10:23 AM	3.20	11	196	1.34	273	0	105	0
1:17:56 AM	1.98	12	197	1.52	327	0	116	0
1:17:58 AM	0.84	13	208	1.72	377	0	116	0
1:20:22 AM	0.60	14	200	1.95	339	0	120	0

Figure 70. Beginning of Simulation

The number of cars waiting at the light (per lane per direction) is shown in this next figure:

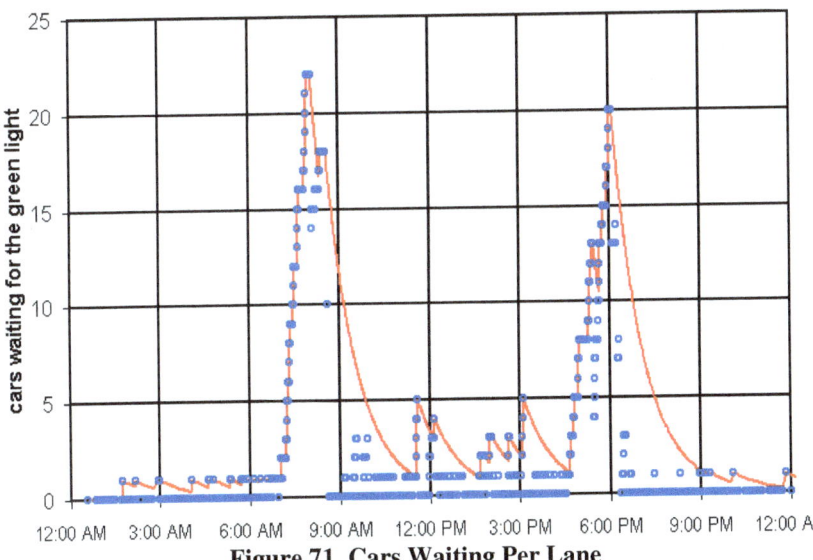

Figure 71. Cars Waiting Per Lane

Here we see the maximum number of cars waiting at the light is 22 in the morning rush, 5 during the noontime, and 20 during the evening rush, which is not at all unreasonable. This could just as well be items waiting to be packaged, packages waiting to be sorted, or delivers waiting to be made.

We can also calculate the wait duration or the amount of time required for each car to pass through the intersection:

77

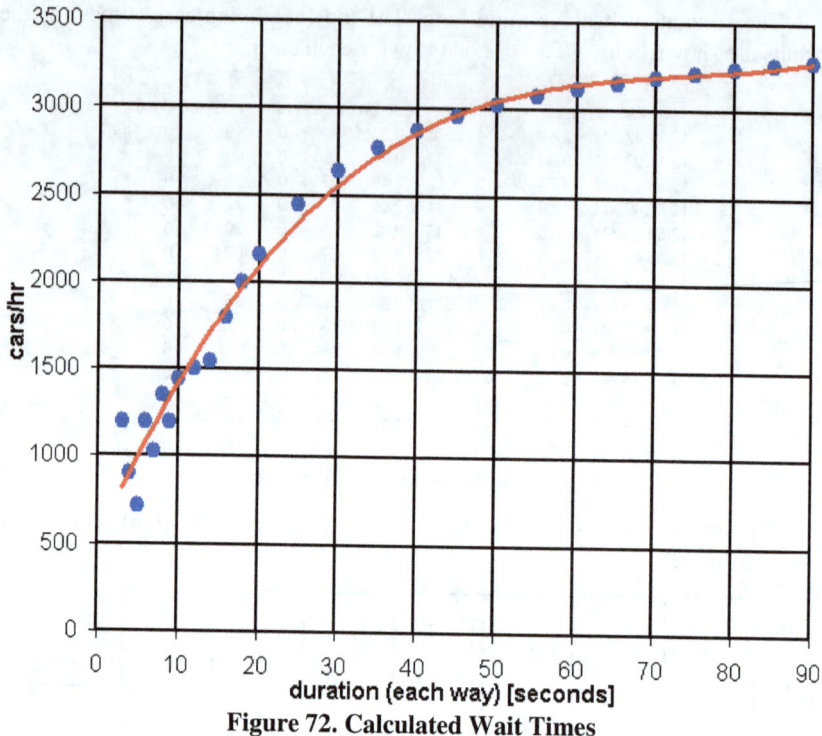
Figure 72. Calculated Wait Times

All of the details may be found in the spreadsheet traffic.xls in the online archive.

Chapter 11. Complex Problems

The first complex problem we will consider is staffing a bi-lingual call center, shown below (details in CallCenter.xls). The time of day is divided into hours (see column A). The calls may be in English or Spanish. The entering calls are user-defined (see magenta cells). Some of the staff only speak English (and get paid $20/hr), while the others are bi-lingual (and get paid $25/hr). The hourly rates are user-defined (see cells highlighted in cyan). Some of the employees are full time and some are part time (see corresponding columns). The employees must not only answer calls but also fill out related paperwork (see corresponding columns).

												Staffing A Call Center													
					English								Spanish												
					full-time				part			full-time													
	incoming		begin		begin		time		begin		begin			avail.staff		max.calls									
shift	Eng	Spa	answering		paperwork				answering		paperwork			Eng	Spn	Eng	Spn	payroll							
7am-9am	32	8	6					2						6	2	36	12	$ 170							
9am-11am	68	17	12		0				3		0			12	3	72	18	$ 315							
11am-1pm	56	14	6	4	0				2	2	0			10	4	60	24	$ 300							
1pm-3pm	76	19	12	1 0	0				3	2 0	0			13	5	78	30	$ 385							
3pm-5pm	64	16	4		0	2 5			2		0		1	11	3	66	18	$ 295							
5pm-7pm	28	7		1	0	5 0			2		0			6	2	36	12	$ 170							
7pm-9pm	8	2				2	0						1	2	1	12	6	$ 65							
begin shift at	7 9 11		1 7 9 11		1 3 5 7 9 11				1 7 9 11 1								total	$1,700							
number	6 12 4		1 0 0		0 2 5 0 2 3 2 2 0 0 0 1																				
employees	English		Spanish	total																					
full-time	25	$ 20	10	$25	35																				
part-time	5		0		5																				

Figure 73. Bi-Lingual Call Center

The shifts are divided into answering calls and filling out paperwork plus depend on whether the employee is full-time or part-time. The corresponding category of employee begins their shift as indicated on row 13 (just above the yellow cells) The number of employees available in each block varies (see cells highlighted in yellow) and are the variables adjusted so as to minimize the payroll (see cell highlighted in green) or minimize the staff required to answer the required (specified) number of calls with the least idle time. The user can change any of the values in the magenta or cyan cells.

Most of the cells are calculated (click on the cell in the spreadsheet to see the respective formulas). The available staff (English and Spanish) is shown for each period in columns V and W. The maximum number of calls each group can handle is shown in columns X and Y. The Solver setup is shown in this next figure:

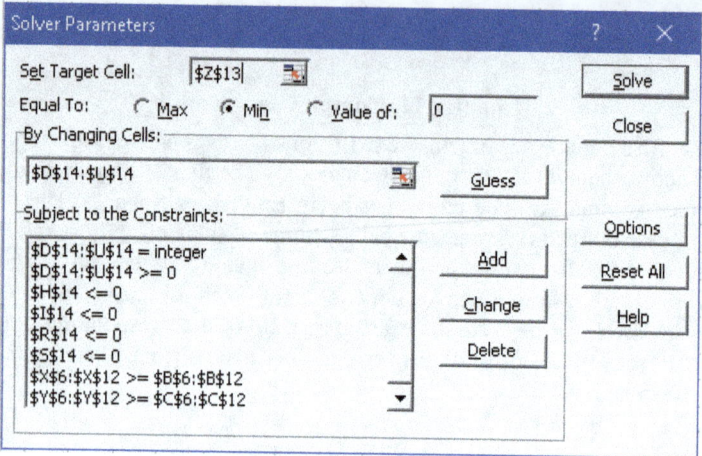

Figure 74. Solver Setup for Call Center

The cell to be optimized is Z13 (the total payroll). The minimum is desired (•)Mi<u>n</u>. The variables to be adjusted are D14:U14. Note that these must all be integers (as you can't have a fraction of an employee). The integer requirement is the first item in the Constraints box. [Note: This is a very convenient feature available with Excel.] These must also be greater than or equal to zero, as indicated in the next line. [You can't have negative employees.]

Cells H14, I14, R14, and S14 must be less than or equal to zero, as these are the "slack" count and would represent a mismatch of workload and staff. The last two lines

```
$X$6:$X$12≥$B$6:$B$12
$Y$6:$Y$12≥$C$6:$C$12
```

require that the maximum number of calls the staff can handle meets or exceeds the incoming calls. This problem takes several seconds to solve. As it does so, you can watch the values in the yellow and green cells change. The final result is shown at the bottom (cells D17:D18 and G17:G18), which indicate 25 full-time and 5 part-time English-speaking employees plus 10 full-time and 0 (no) part-time Spanish-speaking employees are required to staff the Call Center. The total payroll is $1700 per shift.

Cafeteria Problem

We next consider a cafeteria problem in which we must cut costs while meeting nutritional targets. In order to achieve this we can vary the proportion of potatoes and green beans. While the green beans are more nutritious, they are also much more expensive than the potatoes. [Whether or not the kids will eat them all is, of course, a different problem altogether.]

The problem is shown in the following figure and can be found in the cafeteria.xls spreadsheet.

	A	B	C	D	E	F	G	H	I	J
1				Cutting Cafeteria Costs						
2			cost		nutrition/unit			total nutrition		
3			unit	total	protein	iron	Vit.C	protein	iron	Vit.C
4	ingredients	[lb]	[$/lb]	[$]	[gm/lb]	[mg/lb]	[mg/lb]	[gm]	[mg]	[mg]
5	potatoes	13.6	$0.40	$ 5.43	6.8	1.4	54.4	92	18	738
6	green beans	11.3	$1.00	$11.31	9.1	5.4	61.4	103	62	694
7	total	24.9		$16.73	total cost		total	195	80	1432
8	target	22.0					target	180	80	1050
9			taste ratio							
10			[potatoes/greenbean]							
11		actual	1.20							
12		ideal	1.20							

Figure 75. Cafeteria Problem

The unit price is a user input in cells C5:C6 for potatoes and green beans, respectively (highlighted in magenta). The protein, iron, and vitamin C per pound for each are also user inputs (cells E5:G6), also highlighted in magenta. The target weight of both is in cell C8 (highlighted in cyan), as are the target total grams of protein, iron, and vitamin C (cells H8:J8), also highlighted in cyan. The cost is calculated in cell D7 (highlighted in green), which is to be minimized. The remaining cells are calculated (click on each cell in the spreadsheet to see the respective formulas). The Solver is shown in this next figure:

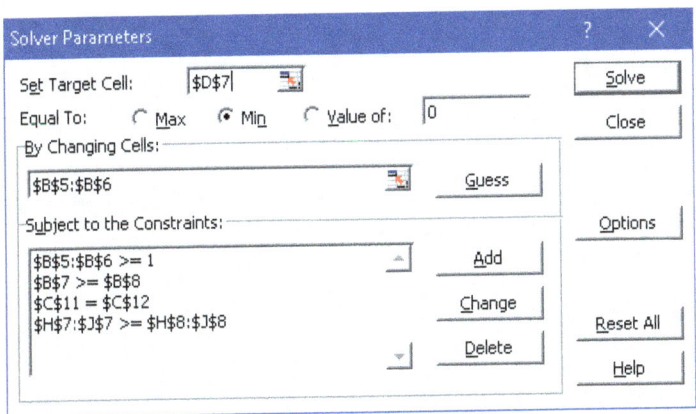

Figure 76. Cafeteria Solver

The target cell is D7 and the (•)Min is selected. The variables are B5:B6. The constraints are first the pounds of each must be greater than or equal to one (≥1). Next the potatoes are greater than or equal to the green beans. Next the overall student taste (demand) target must be met (potatoes to green beans =

81

1.2:1.0). Lastly, the target grams of protein, iron, and vitamin C must be met. The solution is not required to be integers. The Solver can find the solution quickly from any reasonable starting values, which is shown here to be 13.6 pounds of potatoes and 11.3 pounds of green beans.

Bussing Students

In this next example we include several "tricks". The basic idea is bussing students from multiple areas to multiple schools according to some constraints and meeting some objectives while ultimately minimizing cost. This example may be found in the spreadsheet bussing.xls in the online archive. The basic problem is shown in this first figure:

	A	B	C	D	E	F	G	H	I	J
1				Assigning Students To Schools						
2				Percent by Grade			Number by Grade			
3	Area	Students	6th	7th	8th	6th	7th	8th		
4	1	450	32%	38%	30%	144	171	135		
5	2	600	37%	28%	35%	222	168	210		
6	3	550	30%	32%	38%	165	176	209		
7	4	350	28%	40%	32%	98	140	112		
8	5	500	39%	34%	27%	195	170	135		
9	6	450	34%	28%	38%	153	126	171		
10	total	2900			total	977	951	972		
11				Students from Each Area in Each Grade by School						
12		6th Grade Students			7th Grade Students			8th Grade Students		
13	Area	School 1	School 2	School 3	School 1	School 2	School 3	School 1	School 2	School 3
14	1	64	80	0	57	62	52	67	64	4
15	2	0	62	160	0	62	106	0	64	146
16	3	67	62	36	59	63	54	67	64	78
17	4	7	91	0	5	135	0	4	108	0
18	5	67	0	128	66	0	104	67	0	68
19	6	67	62	24	69	57	0	67	64	40
20	total	272	358	347	257	379	315	271	363	338
21		Students by Grade and School				Percent by Grade and School				
22		School 1	School 2	School 3	total		School 1	School 2	School 3	
23	6th Grade	272	358	347	977	6th Grade	34%	33%	35%	
24	7th Grade	257	379	315	951	7th Grade	32%	34%	32%	
25	8th Grade	271	363	338	972	8th Grade	34%	33%	34%	
26	total	800	1100	1000	2900					
27	capacity	900	1100	1000	1000					

Figure 77. Bussing Problem Part 1

The number of students in each grade and area are user inputs cells B4:D9 (highlighted in magenta). The students in 8th grade is calculated (to make up 100% total). The variables are shown in yellow and listed below:

```
B14,C14,E14,F14,H14,I14
C15,F15,I15
B16,C16,E16,F16,H16,I16
B17,E17,H17
B18,E18,H18
B19,C19,E19,F19,H19,I19
```

which is basically how many ride each bus. The gaps (white among yellow cells) in this region (B14:J18) are calculated from the others so as to match the required totals. The number of students bussed to each school is calculated in cells B23:E26. The capacity of each school are user inputs (constraints) in cells B27:D27 (highlighted in cyan). The percent in each grade at each school is a

82

loose constraint (we want some reasonable distribution but it doesn't have to equal a specific value). These cells are also highlighted in cyan. This is one of the "tricks". The problem is continued in this next figure:

	A	B	C	D	E	F	G
28		**Bussing Cost per Student**					
29	**Area**	**School 1**	**School 2**	**School 3**			
30	1	$ 300	$ 0	$ 700			
31	2	#######	$ 400	$ 500			
32	3	$ 600	$ 300	$ 200			
33	4	$ 200	$ 500	########			
34	5	$ 0	########	$ 400			
35	6	$ 500	$ 300	$ 0			
36				**Cost of Bussing**			
37		**Students from Each Area**			**Cost by School and Area**		
38	**Area**	**School 1**	**School 2**	**School 3**	**School 1**	**School 2**	**School 3**
39	1	188	206	56	$ 56,338	$ 0	$ 39,430
40	2	0	188	412	$ –	$ 75,369	$ 205,788
41	3	193	189	168	$ 115,829	$ 56,765	$ 33,547
42	4	16	334	0	$ 3,294	$ 166,766	$ –
43	5	200	0	300	$ 0	$ –	$ 120,107
44	6	203	183	64	$ 101,488	$ 54,879	$ 0
45	**total**	800	1100	1000	$ 276,948	$ 353,780	$ 398,872
46							**$ 1,029,601**

Figure 78. Bussing Problem Part 2

The cost of bussing per student from each of the three areas to each of the three schools are user inputs in cells B30:D35 (mostly highlighted in magenta). The students in Area 5 are close to School 1 (hence the zero in cell B34), as are the students in Area 1 to School 2 (cell C30), and the students in area 6 to School 3 (cell D35). The next "trick" is the cells highlighted in purple (B31, C34, and D33). These costs are set to $10,000,000 per student. This ridiculously high price will assure that no student from Area 2 is bussed to School 1, or from Area 5 to School 2, or from Area 4 to School 3.

The rest of the cells are calculated with the total cost of bussing in cell G46, which we hope to minimize. The Solver is shown in this next figure:

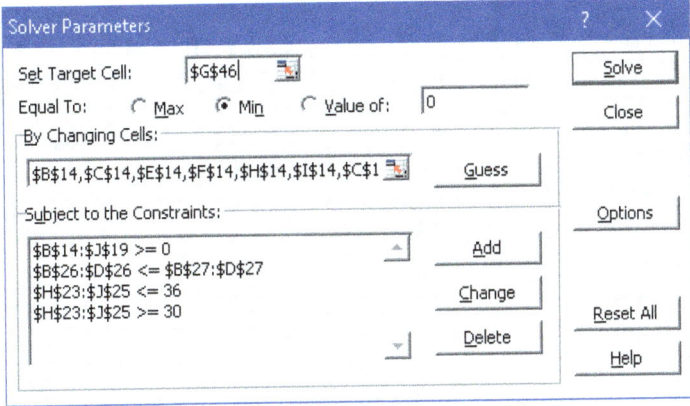

Figure 79. Solver for Bussing Problem

83

The Solver may have considerable difficulty finding the optimum values if the initial guesses are not at least reasonable. We see the result above has achieved an overall cost of $1,029,601. If the Solver fails to find a solution, try changing some of the selections on the Options tab. The "evolutionary" option available with newer versions of Excel is likely the best choice for this problem.

Cost of Opinion Surveys

We next consider the cost of taking a survey. Using information from past experience plus targets provided by the customer wanting the survey results, you must come up with an estimate and ultimately a competitive bid. The problem and details can be found in spreadsheet survey.xls in the online archive and is shown below:

	A	B	C	D	E	F	G	H	I	J	K	L	M
1		Cost by Age Group and Locale				People in Each Category				total by	percent	target	total
2	Region	18-25	26-40	41-50	51-99	18-25	26-40	41-50	51-99	region	region	percent	cost
3	Silicon Valley	$4.75	$6.50	$6.50	$5.00	500	50	50	200	800	40%	15.0%	$ 4,025
4	Big Cities	$5.25	$5.75	$6.25	$6.25	150	450	50	50	700	35%	35.0%	$ 4,000
5	Small Towns	$6.50	$7.50	$7.50	$7.25	200	50	200	50	500	25%	25.0%	$ 3,537
6				total by age group		850	550	300	300	2000		total	$11,562
7				percent by age group		42.5%	27.5%	15.0%	15.0%	2000	target	profit	$ 1,734
8				target percentage		20.0%	27.5%	15.0%	15.0%		surveys	bid	$13,297

Figure 80. Cost of Conducting a Survey

The estimated cost per person is divided into four age groups (18-25, 26-40, 41-50, and 51-99) and three locations (Silicon Valley, Big Cities, and Small Towns). These are all user inputs in cells B3:E5, highlighted in magenta. The differences could arise from a number of factors, including how chatty people are where and by age or how many times you must repeat and explain the questions. You could extract such factors if you kept a record of previous surveys and performed multivariate regression, as illustrated in the second half of Chapter 9.

The number of people surveyed in each category are the variables adjusted so as to meet the objectives. These are in cells F3:I5, highlighted in yellow. There are several objectives or requirements (presumably set by the customer paying for the survey). The first of these is the target percentages by location, which are in cells L3:L5, highlighted in cyan. The target percentages by age group are in cells F8:I8, also highlighted in cyan. The target number of people surveyed is also a requirement. This is in cell J7, highlighted in cyan.

All of the other cells are calculated, including the count, percentage, and totals, along with costs associated with each and total cost. You can click on each cell to see the formula. The total cost is shown at the bottom right in cell M8, highlighted in green. We seek the solution (yellow cells) that yield the smallest cost (green cell), while satisfying the constraints (cyan cells).

The Solver setup looks like this:

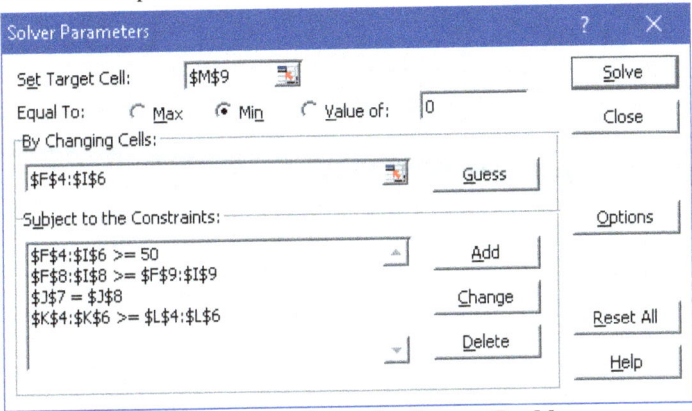

Figure 81. Solver Setup for Survey Problem

Here we see the target cell is M9 and the (•)Min is sought. The variables changed (adjusted) to achieve this are F4:I6. The constraints include: 1) at least 50 in each category; 2) at least the minimum target percentages in each age group; 3) the target total number of people surveyed; and 4) at least the target percentages in each location group. The solution is $13,297 and so the price agreed upon must meet or exceed this amount.

Making Clothes

We next consider a more complex clothing manufacture problem. In this case we have seven materials (fabrics) used in the production: acetate, cashmere, cotton, rayon, silk, velvet, and wool. The available quantities (in yards) and cost (per yard) are user inputs in cells B3:C9, highlighted in magenta, as shown in this first figure:

	A	B	C	D
1	material cost and availability			
2	material	yards	per yard	material
3	acetate	28,000	$1.50	$42,000
4	cashmere	9,000	$60.00	$540,000
5	cotton	30,000	$2.50	$75,000
6	rayon	30,000	$2.25	$67,500
7	silk	18,000	$13.00	$234,000
8	velvet	20,000	$12.00	$240,000
9	wool	45,000	$9.00	$405,000
10	total	180,000		$1,603,500

Figure 82. List of Materials (Fabrics)

85

Using these seven fabrics we manufacture eleven different products: cashmere sweater, cotton miniskirt, cotton sweater, rayon blouse, rayon skirt, silk blouse, silk skirt, velvet pants, velvet shirt, wool blazer, and wool slacks, as shown in this next figure:

	F	G	H	I	J	K	L	M	N
1		material required per item made							
2	item	acetate	cashmere	cotton	rayon	silk	velvet	wool	total
3	cashmere sweater		1.5						1.5
4	cotton miniskirt			0.5					0.5
5	cotton sweater			1.5					1.5
6	rayon blouse				1.5				1.5
7	rayon skirt	1.5			2.0				3.5
8	silk blouse					1.5			1.5
9	silk camisole					0.5			0.5
10	velvet pants	2.0					3.0		5.0
11	velvet shirt						1.5		1.5
12	wool blazer	1.5						2.5	4.0
13	wool slacks	2.0						3.0	5.0

Figure 83. List of Products (Clothing Items)

[I know you're wondering... Yes, I got some help on this one from a relative of a coworker who lives in NYC and works in the garment industry.]

The quantity of each material required for each clothing item are also user inputs in cells G3:M13, highlighted in magenta. Note that acetate is used in several items as a liner. The quantity of each item produced is the solution in cells Q3:Q13, highlighted in yellow. These are all integers, so we check that box in the Solver Options.

	P	Q	R	S	T	U	V	W	X
1		items made and total material required							
2	item	items	acetate	cashmere	cotton	rayon	silk	velvet	wool
3	cashmere sweater	6,000		9,000					
4	cotton miniskirt	60,000			30,000				
5	cotton sweater	0			0				
6	rayon blouse	19,111				28,667			
7	rayon skirt	667	1,000			1,333			
8	silk blouse	12,000					18,000		
9	silk camisole	0					0		
10	velvet pants	0	0					0	
11	velvet shirt	13,333						20,000	
12	wool blazer	18,000	27,000						45,000
13	wool slacks	0	0						0
14	total		28,000	9,000	30,000	30,000	18,000	20,000	45,000
15	unused		0	0	0	0	0	0	0

Figure 84. Quantity of Each Item Produced

The total yards of each material required for each item is calculated in this space (cells R3:X13), as is the total for each material (at the bottom in cells R14:X14). These cells are highlighted in cyan because they are constraints (we can't use more material than we have available, which is in cells B3:B9). The unused (leftover) material is calculated in cells R15:X15, which must be greater than or equal to zero in order to meet the constraints implied by the available material. The labor cost to produce each item are user inputs in cells AA3:AA13, highlighted in magenta in the next figure. The material cost is calculated from the quantity (in yards) and the cost (per yard). The total labor and material for each item is also calculated in these cells, as shown:

	Z	AA	AB	AC	AD	AE	AF
1				cost to produce			
2	item	labor	material	each	labor	material	total
3	cashmere sweater	$150	$90.00	$240.00	$900,000	$540,000	$1,440,000
4	cotton miniskirt	$40	$1.25	$41.25	$2,400,000	$75,000	$2,475,000
5	cotton sweater	$60	$3.75	$63.75	$0	$0	$0
6	rayon blouse	$45	$3.38	$48.38	$860,000	$64,500	$924,500
7	rayon skirt	$45	$6.75	$51.75	$30,000	$4,500	$34,500
8	silk blouse	$50	$19.50	$69.50	$600,000	$234,000	$834,000
9	silk camisole	$60	$6.50	$66.50	$0	$0	$0
10	velvet pants	$175	$18.00	$193.00	$0	$0	$0
11	velvet shirt	$160	$18.00	$178.00	$2,133,333	$240,000	$2,373,333
12	wool blazer	$140	$24.75	$164.75	$2,520,000	$445,500	$2,965,500
13	wool slacks	$160	$30.00	$190.00	$0	$0	$0
14				total	$9,443,333	$1,603,500	$11,046,833

Figure 85. Cost to Produce Each Item

The wholesale price of each item is a user input in cells AI3:AI13, highlighted below in magenta. The profit for each item in dollars and percentage as well as the total for that item are calculated in the cells below with the total profit summed at the bottom in cell AL14.

	AH	AI	AJ	AK	AL
1			profit		
2	item	price	profit	profit	profit
3	cashmere sweater	$300	$60	20%	$360,000
4	cotton miniskirt	$60	$19	31%	$1,125,000
5	cotton sweater	$90	$26	29%	$0
6	rayon blouse	$60	$12	19%	$222,167
7	rayon skirt	$75	$23	31%	$15,500
8	silk blouse	$145	$76	52%	$906,000
9	silk camisole	$75	$9	11%	$0
10	velvet pants	$225	$32	14%	$0
11	velvet shirt	$200	$22	11%	$293,333
12	wool blazer	$200	$35	18%	$634,500
13	wool slacks	$225	$35	16%	$0
14					$3,556,500

Figure 86. Profit

We set up the Solver accordingly, as shown in this next figure:

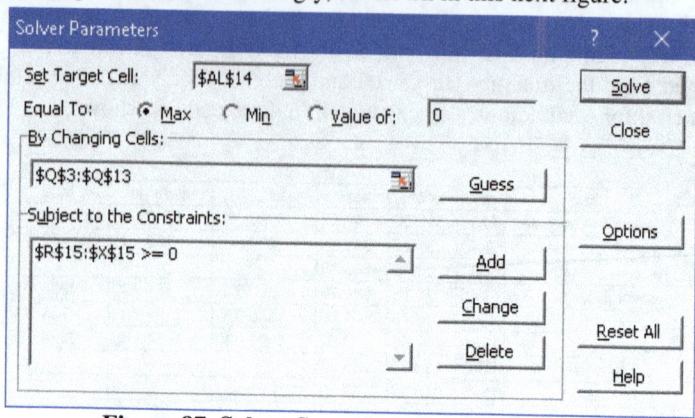

Figure 87. Solver Setup for Clothing Problem

The target cell is AL14 (total net profit), the (•)Max is desired, the variables (number of each item produced) are cells Q3:Q13, and the constraints are the unused (leftover) yards of each material in cells R15:X14, which must be greater than or equal to zero.

We see in the preceding table that the maximum net profit is achieved by producing 6,000 cashmere sweaters, 60,000 cotton miniskirts, 0 cotton sweaters, 19,111 rayon blouses, 667 rayon skirts, 12,000 silk blouses, 0 silk camisoles, 0 velvet pants, 13,333 velvet shirts, 18,000 wool blazers, and 0 wool slacks. It may be unexpected but should not be too surprising that the solution indicates that we should produce none of four items. This is why there are often bare spots on the shelves. The demand exceeds the motivation to produce some items. It also explains why there always seem to be more than enough of some other items we may not choose to purchase. Such is life in the very real world of manufacturing.

Limited Materials

Lack of materials is often a problem in manufacturing, whether due to cost or availability. In this problem acetate is used (as a liner) in making four items: rayon skirt, velvet pants, wool blazer, and wool slacks. If we were to reduce the available amount of acetate from 28,000 to 20,000 yards, the number of items would necessarily have to change, if for no other reason, there was no unused material before.

The impact of decreasing the amount of acetate is shown in this next table:

item	before	after	difference
cashmere sweater	6,000	6,000	0
cotton miniskirt	60,000	60,000	0
cotton sweater	0	0	0
rayon blouse	19,111	20,000	889
rayon skirt	667	0	-667
silk blouse	12,000	12,000	0
silk camisole	0	0	0
velvet pants	0	0	0
velvet shirt	13,333	13,333	0
wool blazer	18,000	13,333	-4,667
wool slacks	0	0	0
	$3,556,500	$3,386,833	-$169,667

Figure 88. Impact of Limited Acetate

The number of rayon blouses increased by 889 from 19,111 to 20,000. The number of rayon skirts decreased from 667 to zero. The number of wool blazers decreased by 4,667 from 18,000 to 13,333. The net profit decreased from $3,556,500 to $3,386,833 for a loss of $169,667. Here we see that less material doesn't necessarily mean that the number of some item may not increase.

Limited Labor

Production is often labor-limited. The original labor cost was $9,433,333. What if we were limited to $8,000,000 in labor (by hours or people or budget)? The impact is listed in this next table:

item	before	after	difference
cashmere sweater	6,000	6,000	0
cotton miniskirt	60,000	60,000	0
cotton sweater	0	0	0
rayon blouse	19,111	19,111	0
rayon skirt	667	667	0
silk blouse	12,000	12,000	0
silk camisole	0	0	0
velvet pants	0	0	0
velvet shirt	13,333	4,313	-9,021
wool blazer	18,000	18,000	0
wool slacks	0	0	0
net profit	$3,556,500	$3,358,042	-$198,458
labor cost	$9,443,333	$8,000,000	-$207,479

Figure 89. Impact of Limited Labor

Note that only the number of velvet shirts produced changed down 9,021 from 13,333 to 4,313. The profit dropped from $3,556,500 to $3,358,042 or a loss of $198,458. The labor cost per velvet shirt is $160, which isn't the most time-consuming item. The labor cost per velvet pants is $175 but the profit margin is higher (14% as compared to 11%). We also have 13,531 yards of velvet left over so this is another unutilized asset that works into the calculations.

What if for some strange reason we wanted to spend at least $10,000,000 on labor. Maybe this is a corporate target to satisfy a union agreement? The result of this target is shown in the following table:

item	before	after	difference
cashmere sweater	6,000	6,000	0
cotton miniskirt	60,000	60,000	0
cotton sweater	0	0	0
rayon blouse	19,111	19,111	0
rayon skirt	667	667	0
silk blouse	12,000	7,718	-4,282
silk camisole	0	12,846	12,846
velvet pants	0	0	0
velvet shirt	13,333	13,333	0
wool blazer	18,000	18,000	0
wool slacks	0	0	0
net profit	$3,556,500	$3,342,397	-$214,103
labor cost	$9,443,333	$10,000,000	-$205,538

Figure 90. Impact of Labor Target

In this case we would have to make 4,282 fewer silk blouses and 12,846 more silk camisoles. The net profit would drop from $3,556,500 to $3,342,397 or a loss of $205,538. Notice that the increased cost of labor is $556,667, which is less than the loss in profit by more than a factor of 2. The union might argue that with more than a 2:1 ratio, cutting back on profit in this way is better for the employees than it is bad for the company.

Meeting Demand

In Chapter 4 we considered the complex problem of when to shift gears. Here we will consider the problem of operating a hybrid solar power plant to meet demand. We begin with actual hourly power demand from DoE (the U.S. Department of Energy) shown here:

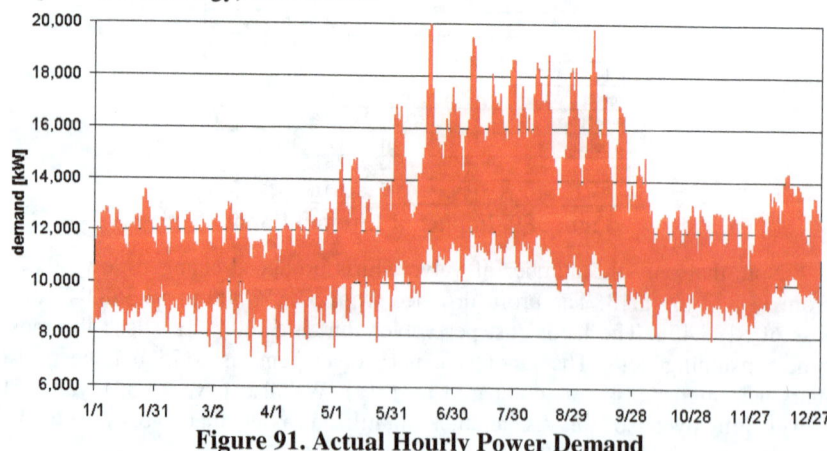

Figure 91. Actual Hourly Power Demand

90

The demand varies between 7,000 to 20,000 kW (kilowatts) but is never zero. This is very important! There is always a demand for electricity and if you don't provide it, the customers will be more than displeased. The challenge we have here is that solar cells only produce power when the sun is shining; therefore, we must have an additional source of power and this other source *must be dispatchable*. We must be able to bring it up and down at will in order to meet demand. In this example we will use a natural gas combustion turbine generator.

Before we can dispatch our gas turbine we must consider how much solar is available. We could get such data from DoE or calculate it based on location and atmospheric clarity. In this case we will calculate the solar using a formula provided by the National Renewable Energy Laboratory: Algorithm for Solar Radiation Applications; NREL Report No. TP-560-34302, 2008. The Excel macro can be found in the spreadsheet (solar.xls), which is available in the online archive. We define the latitude and longitude as user inputs. The clear sky Direct Normal Insolation (DNI) for this same period as the demand data and on an hourly basis is shown in this next figure:

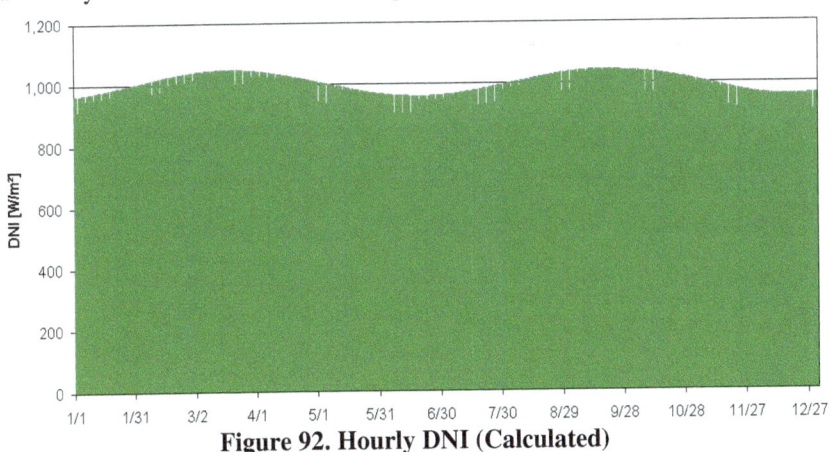

Figure 92. Hourly DNI (Calculated)

Note the annual (seasonal) variation (i.e., winter, spring, summer, fall).

91

The daily variation is shown in this next figure:

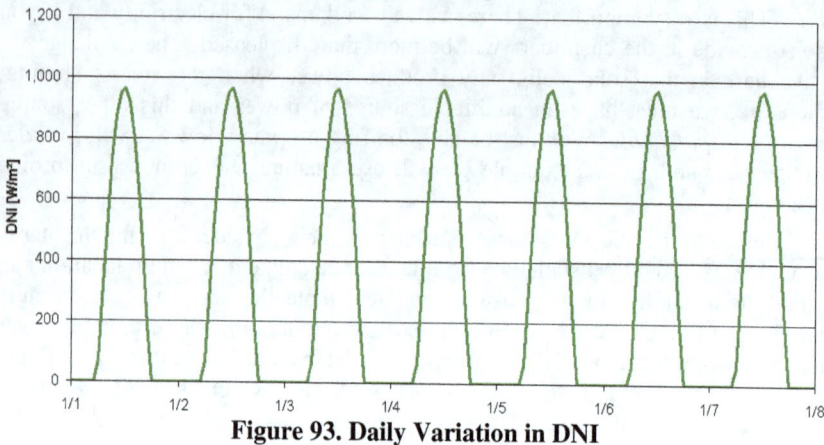

Figure 93. Daily Variation in DNI

Most people unfamiliar with actual data greatly overestimate the clarity of the sky. For reference, we consider actual measured cloudiness in Phoenix, Arizona, a place people associate with clear skies.

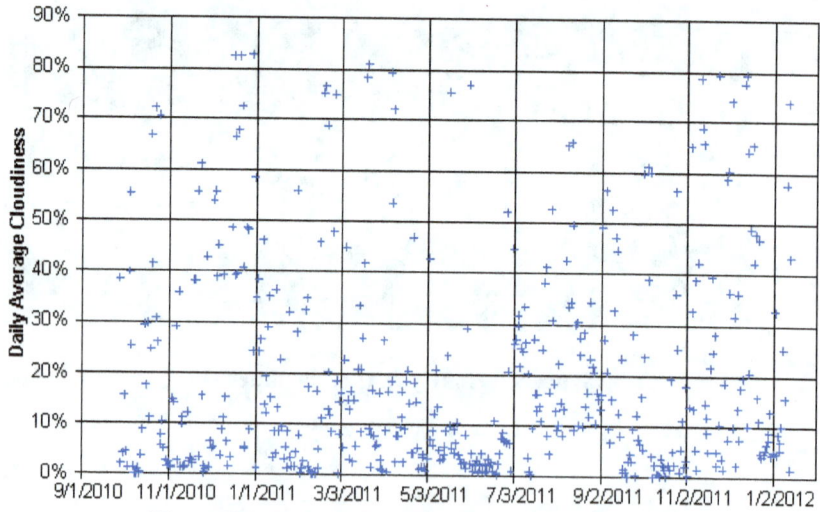

Figure 94. Measured Cloudiness in Phoenix, AZ

Clearly, the skies over Phoenix are not always clear... and neither are they anywhere else...

The statistical measure of this same data is shown in the following figure:

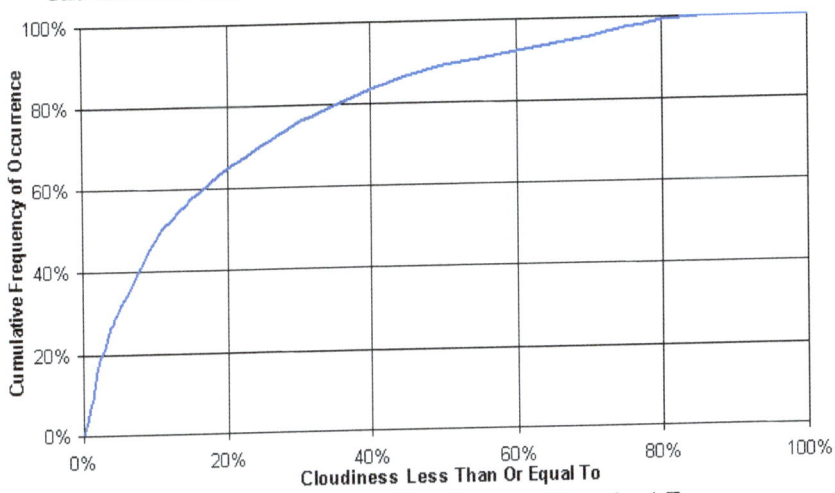

Figure 95. Statistical Cloudiness in Phoenix, AZ

The point of these two figures is: Don't build a solar plant thinking the sky will always be clear or that you will be able to consistently produce the rated output of the solar panels because this won't happen.

For the purposes of this simulation we will approximate the cloudiness as a normally-distributed random number based on the average and standard deviation (both user-defined variables in the spreadsheet) using the same Excel macro as before. The result is shown in the following figure:

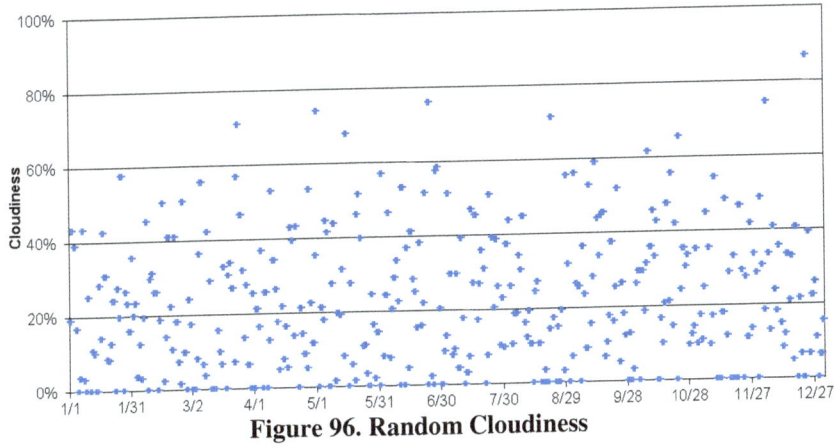

Figure 96. Random Cloudiness

We calculate the net power available each hour from the solar panels from the design (maximum) output times the DNI times the sky clarity, which is equal to one minus the cloudiness. The demand for that hour may be more or less than the available solar. If it is more, the gas turbine will be required. The power that must be supplied by the gas turbine to meet demand is shown in this next figure:

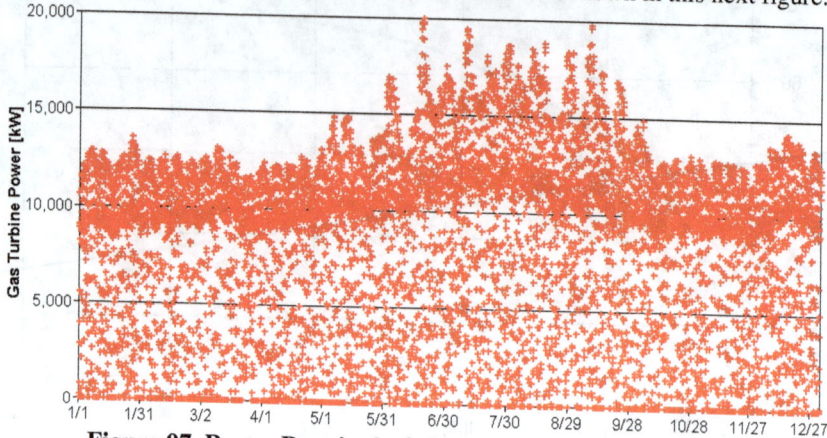

Figure 97. Power Required of Gas Turbine to Meet Demand

The performance of a gas turbine depends on several things, including the weather and the load. For the purposes of this example we will only consider the variation with load. We could get hourly weather data from NOAA near the location of interest and add this to the calculation. Instead, we use a curve for a typical gas turbine. This figure shows the impact of load on heat rate, which is the rate at which fuel must be burned to run the turbine. The fuel flow (and cost) is calculated from the heat rate divided by the heating value of the fuel.

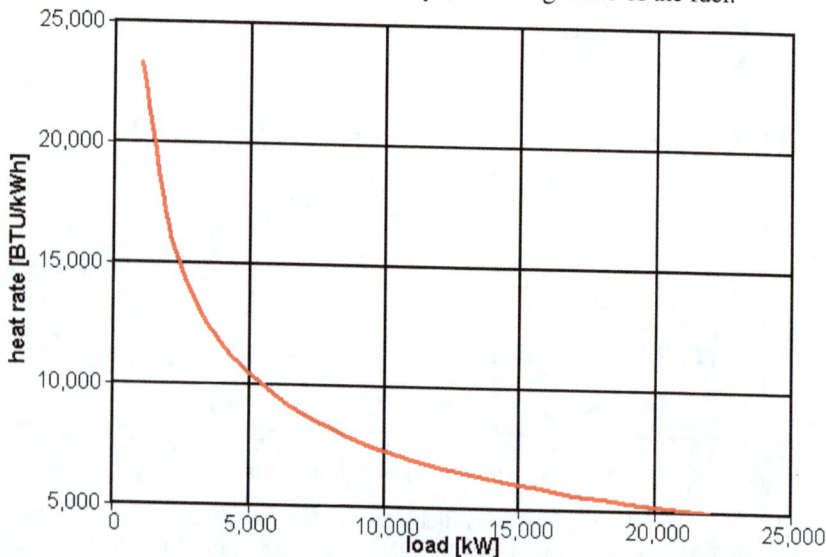

Figure 98. Gas Turbine Heat Rate

94

The percent "green" (fraction of the power derived from solar) is shown in this next figure:

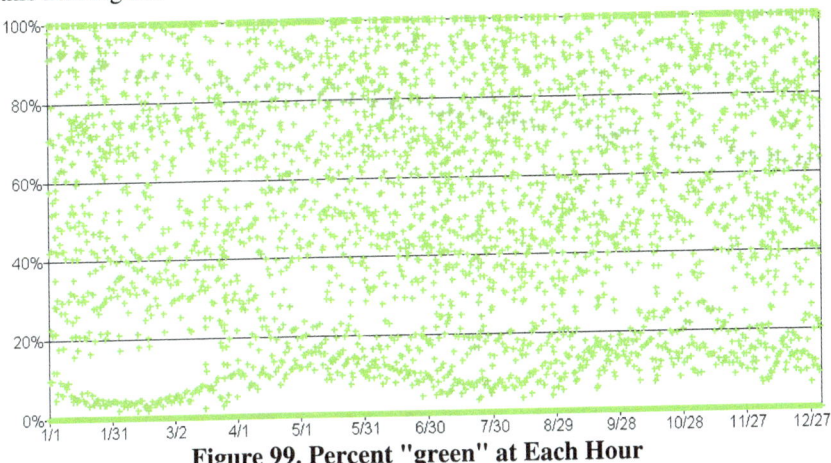

Figure 99. Percent "green" at Each Hour

The overall average "green" for the year is 33%, which is rather high and above what most systems of this type can achieve. We next consider the cost, which is how this simulation fits in with every other industrial process: we must not only produce what is required but we must also be cost-effective or the unavoidable result is failure. Here we consider the following costs: loan (paying for the equipment), fuel (cost of gas), maintenance (cost to keep it running), total cost, revenue (income based on kWh delivered and price per kWh), net profit (at each hour), and the running balance at each hour. There are several user inputs:

	P	Q	R	S
1	input/output parameters			user inputs
2	latitude	35	°North	calculation outputs
3	longitude	-85	°East	rate
4	cloudiness	20%	average	
5	cloudiness	20%	std.dev.	adjust rate
6	reserve	9%	capacity	
7	capacity	21,783	kW	
8	solar cost	$4,000	dollars/kW	
9	GT cost	$800	dollars/kW	
10	total cost	$104,556,288	dollars	
11	lifetime	25	years	
12	interest	6%	/yr	
13	power	$0.15	/kWh	
14	nat. gas	$8	/mmBTU	
15	solar main.	$25	/kWh/yr	
16	GT main.	$75	/kWh/yr	
17	yearly net	$0	dollars	

Figure 100. User Inputs

95

User inputs include: latitude and longitude (for calculating solar position), cloudiness (average and standard deviation), reserve capacity, cost of solar equipment (purchase price) in $/kW, cost of gas turbine in $/kW, expected lifetime (years of service over which to retire debt), interest rate, wholesale price of power, price of natural gas (based on heat content), cost of maintaining the solar panels per kW per year, cost of gas turbine maintenance per kW per year. The sixth value (capacity), ninth value (total cost) and last value (yearly net) in this table are calculated. These values are typical and so yield a reasonable estimate of such an operation. The hour-by-hour simulation looks like this:

	A	B	C	D	E	F	G	H	I	J	K	L	M	N	O
1						model of a combined solar/natural gas turbine power plant									
2	date:time	demand	clear	cloud	solar	green	GT	Ht.Rt.	loan	fuel	maint.	cost	revenue	profit	balance
3		kW	W/m²	%	kW	%	kW	BTU/kWh	$	$	$	$	$	$	$
4	1/1/2021 0:00	10,591	0	21%	0	0%	10,591	7,171	$1,045	$608	$249	$1,901	$1,630	-$271	-$271
5	1/1/2021 1:00	10,591	0	21%	0	0%	10,591	7,171	$1,045	$608	$249	$1,901	$1,630	-$271	-$542
6	1/1/2021 2:00	10,591	0	21%	0	0%	10,591	7,171	$1,045	$608	$249	$1,901	$1,630	-$271	-$813
7	1/1/2021 3:00	8,981	0	21%	0	0%	8,981	7,787	$1,045	$559	$249	$1,853	$1,382	-$471	-$1,284
8	1/1/2021 4:00	8,831	0	21%	0	0%	8,831	7,853	$1,045	$555	$249	$1,848	$1,359	-$489	-$1,773
9	1/1/2021 5:00	8,843	0	21%	0	0%	8,843	7,847	$1,045	$555	$249	$1,849	$1,361	-$488	-$2,261
10	1/1/2021 6:00	9,050	69	21%	873	10%	8,177	8,160	$1,045	$534	$249	$1,827	$1,393	-$435	-$2,695
11	1/1/2021 7:00	9,466	316	21%	3,984	42%	5,482	9,967	$1,045	$437	$249	$1,731	$1,457	-$274	-$2,969
12	1/1/2021 8:00	9,658	542	21%	6,824	71%	2,834	13,861	$1,045	$314	$249	$1,608	$1,487	-$121	-$3,091
13	1/1/2021 9:00	9,399	731	21%	9,199	98%	200	52,211	$1,045	$83	$249	$1,377	$1,447	$70	-$3,021
14	1/1/2021 10:00	8,958	870	21%	8,958	100%	0	N/A	$1,045	$0	$249	$1,294	$1,379	$85	-$2,936
15	1/1/2021 11:00	8,592	949	21%	8,592	100%	0	N/A	$1,045	$0	$249	$1,294	$1,322	$29	-$2,907
16	1/1/2021 12:00	8,392	964	21%	8,392	100%	0	N/A	$1,045	$0	$249	$1,294	$1,292	-$2	-$2,909
17	1/1/2021 13:00	8,383	914	21%	8,383	100%	0	N/A	$1,045	$0	$249	$1,294	$1,290	-$3	-$2,912
18	1/1/2021 14:00	8,479	801	21%	8,479	100%	0	N/A	$1,045	$0	$249	$1,294	$1,305	$11	-$2,901
19	1/1/2021 15:00	8,749	633	21%	7,976	91%	773	26,540	$1,045	$164	$249	$1,458	$1,347	-$111	-$3,012
20	1/1/2021 16:00	9,237	423	21%	5,325	58%	3,912	11,798	$1,045	$369	$249	$1,663	$1,422	-$241	-$3,253
21	1/1/2021 17:00	10,211	184	21%	2,311	23%	7,900	8,303	$1,045	$525	$249	$1,818	$1,572	-$247	-$3,500
22	1/1/2021 18:00	11,421	0	21%	0	0%	11,421	6,905	$1,045	$631	$249	$1,925	$1,758	-$167	-$3,667
23	1/1/2021 19:00	11,578	0	21%	0	0%	11,578	6,858	$1,045	$635	$249	$1,929	$1,782	-$147	-$3,814
24	1/1/2021 20:00	11,451	0	21%	0	0%	11,451	6,896	$1,045	$632	$249	$1,925	$1,762	-$163	-$3,977
25	1/1/2021 21:00	11,157	0	21%	0	0%	11,157	6,986	$1,045	$624	$249	$1,917	$1,717	-$200	-$4,176
26	1/1/2021 22:00	10,787	0	21%	0	0%	10,787	7,105	$1,045	$613	$249	$1,907	$1,660	-$246	-$4,423
27	1/1/2021 23:00	10,177	0	21%	0	0%	10,177	7,315	$1,045	$596	$249	$1,889	$1,566	-$323	-$4,746

Figure 101. Hour-by-Hour Simulation

The button [adjust rate] shown in the previous figure beside the user inputs launches a macro that adjust the wholesale price (we must get) in order to break even (i.e., the net balance in the far right column at the end of the year equal to zero). This is the "break even" number. If we can't get at least this much, the plant is not viable.

Chapter 12. Optimizing Multiple Targets

As in life, the demands of business are not always reasonable, nor the decisions clear. Not every industrial process will lend itself to simple mathematical solution. Sometimes you are given directives that seem logically and even mathematically impossible. No offence intended here, but math majors rarely end up in management, so decision makers may not always think in clear cut mathematical terms. That's when we technical types must become even more creative...

Let's say you have been compiling data from the widget factory for some time and have come up with some very interesting graphs, including net profit (items made times wholesale price less costs and flaws) and net items produced (less flaws and rejections) so have created the following graph of which you are very proud.

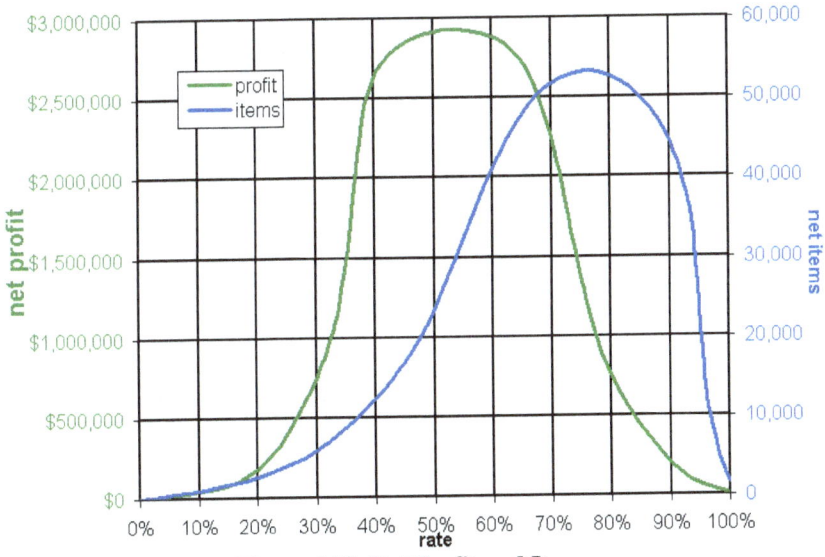

Figure 102. Net Profit and Items

You show this to the Boss, who says, "Excellent! Now go out there and optimize profit *and* productivity!"

You almost spew coffee on the Boss then struggle to explain, "Net profit peaks at 53% but net items peaks at 76%. It's not possible to optimize both."

The concept flies right over the Boss' head, who pats you on the shoulder says, "Great! Let's make this the best quarter yet," turns, and walks away.

So... what do you do? While this might seem like a silly problem in an industrial setting, it's not all that different from other challenges in life. How do you optimize the kid's health, run all the errands, show up at work on time, plan a vacation, and stay within the budget? Sometimes we must juggle different things with different measures. In this case we must somehow combine profit and items produced. One is dollars and the other is widgets. If we must decide on a single combined optimum, what we need is a relationship between the two.

Here is one approach... Say to the Boss, "Close your eyes and put out your hands. Imagine you have profits in your left hand and widgets in your right. Now move them up and down, getting a feel for their relative weight. Are they of equal importance 50/50 or are profits more like 80/20 or widgets more like 20/80?" Watch the hands and come up with a relative importance or proportional weight. Use this to create an effective combined value of the two. In this example we take the average profit for one widget of $55 and create a fourth column. The result is:

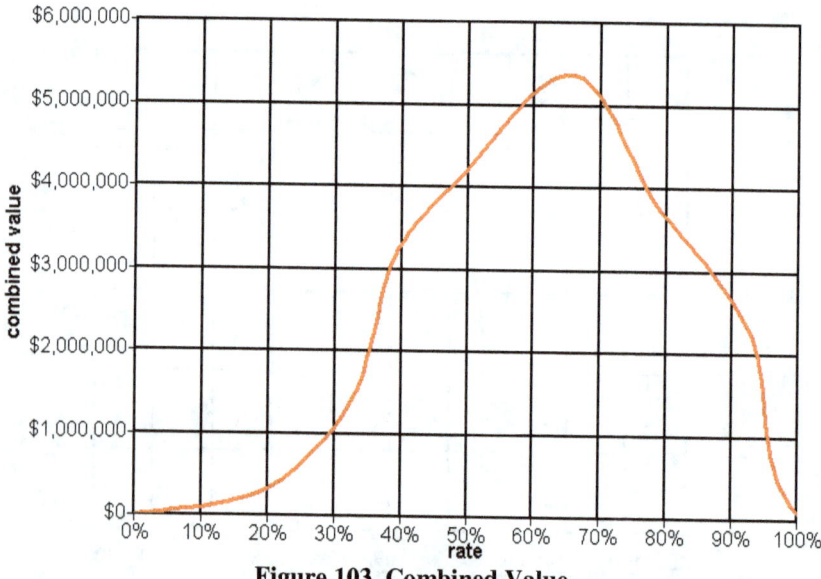

Figure 103. Combined Value

The peak combined value occurs at 67%, which, not surprisingly, is between the two previous peaks. This same concept works with three, four, or even more seemingly competing or incompatible targets. This method (combining two or more results using weighting factors to arrive at a composite value) works with Excel's Solver too. If we revisit one of the spreadsheets where we adjust some operational factor, which, in turn, changes the number of

98

widgets, flaws, cost, and/or profit, we can create an additional cell where we calculate the composite objective and redirect the Solver to maximize or minimize this by changing the controls. In this case we combined two positives. We have already considered subtracting flaws from total widgets to get net widgets. We can do the same with negative items (flaws, increased maintenance, increased labor, machine down time, etc.). The final result doesn't have to be a positive number. We might seek the least negative composite result, which would still be a maximum to the Solver.

We have already considered the problem when increased rate of production results in more flaws or items not meeting tolerance specs, as illustrated in this next figure. We revisit this problem with a twist.

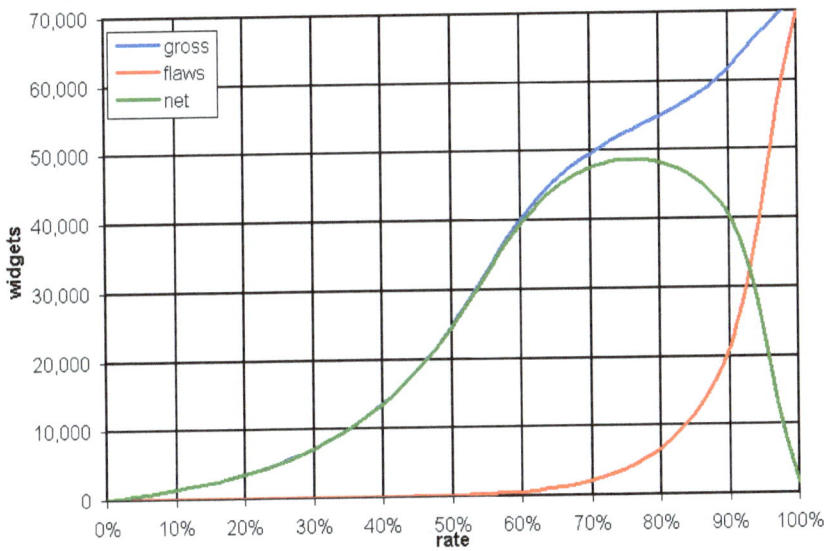

Figure 104. Total, Flaws, and Net Widgets

What if instead of widgets we were making pacemakers or heart valves or bombs? What if a flawed item might explode or release contamination or at least require special attention such as cessation of production donning hazmat suits and removing it from the premises? This is not an unreasonable scenario. The Y-12 nuclear weapons plant is just up the road from my home, as was the entire K-25 uranium enrichment facility. In fact, I helped clean up some of the messes left over after the Manhattan Project.

Flaws are unavoidable but in such cases we hope to keep these to a minimum. The only way to assure there will never be a workplace accident is to close the plant and send everyone home. That's not an option in most cases. It certainly was not an option during the Manhattan Project. So how do we approach a problem like this? One way would be what we've just been discussing; which is to *weight* the flaws. In such cases one flaw isn't the same as one less nuclear warhead out the door. That one flaw represents a potential disaster. Closing the factory and sending everyone home is mathematically equivalent to an infinite weight. Put another way, if no flaws are acceptable there will be no production. We must, therefore, consider a finite weight in order to arrive at an acceptable solution and still produce something. If we have collected the data and built a spreadsheet we can quickly and easily consider such scenarios and calculate optimums. For the purposes of illustration we will simply multiply the flaws by 20 to indicate the excess effort. The result is shown in this last figure:

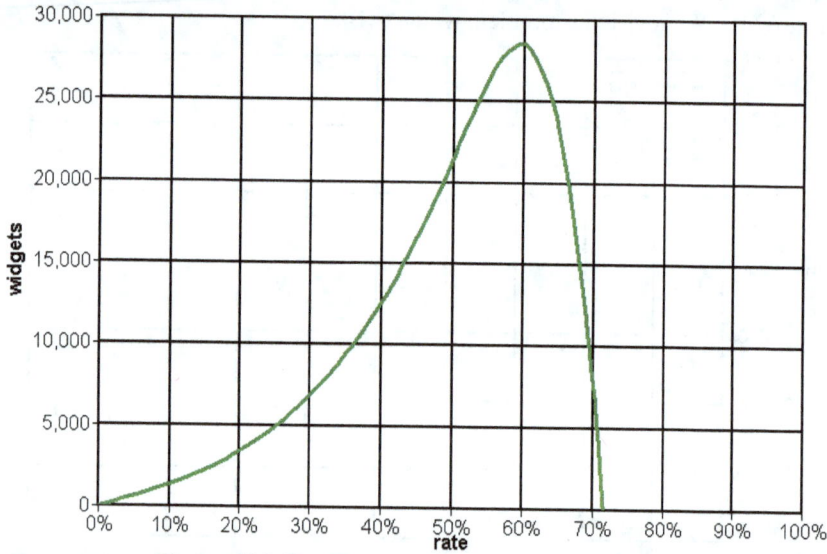

Figure 105. Result Considering Weighted Flaws

The new optimum occurs at 60% production rate. No doubt those working on the Manhattan Project struggled with such decisions but didn't have computers or spreadsheets or Excel or color printers or PowerPoint to present the results.

also by D. James Benton

3D Articulation: Using OpenGL, ISBN-9798596362480, Amazon, 2021 (book 3 in the 3D series).

3D Models in Motion Using OpenGL, ISBN-9798652987701, Amazon, 2020 (book 2 in the 3D series.

3D Rendering in Windows: How to display three-dimensional objects in Windows with and without OpenGL, ISBN-9781520339610, Amazon, 2016 (book 1 in the 3D series).

A Synergy of Short Stories: The whole may be greater than the sum of the parts, ISBN-9781520340319, Amazon, 2016.

Azeotropes: Behavior and Application, ISBN-9798609748997, Amazon, 2020.

bat-Elohim: Book 3 in the Little Star Trilogy, ISBN-9781686148682, Amazon, 2019.

Blind Love: Like A Tiger, ISBN-9798343761610, Amazon, 2024.

Boilers: Performance and Testing, ISBN: 9798789062517, Amazon, 2021.

Combined 3D Rendering Series: 3D Rendering in Windows®, 3D Models in Motion, and 3D Articulation, ISBN-9798484417032, Amazon, 2021.

Complex Variables: Practical Applications, ISBN-9781794250437, Amazon, 2019.

Compression & Encryption: Algorithms & Software, ISBN-9781081008826, Amazon, 2019.

Computational Fluid Dynamics: an Overview of Methods, ISBN-9781672393775, Amazon, 2019.

Computer Simulation of Power Systems: Programming Strategies and Practical Examples, ISBN-9781696218184, Amazon, 2019.

Contaminant Transport: A Numerical Approach, ISBN-9798461733216, Amazon, 2021.

CPUnleashed! Tapping Processor Speed, ISBN-9798421420361, Amazon, 2022.

Curve-Fitting: The Science and Art of Approximation, ISBN-9781520339542, Amazon, 2016.

Death by Tie: It was the best of ties. It was the worst of ties. It's what got him killed., ISBN-9798398745931, Amazon, 2023.

Differential Equations: Numerical Methods for Solving, ISBN-9781983004162, Amazon, 2018.

Equations of State: A Graphical Comparison, ISBN-9798843139520, Amazon, 2022.

Evaporative Cooling: The Science of Beating the Heat, ISBN-9781520913346, Amazon, 2017.

Forecasting: Extrapolation and Projection, ISBN-9798394019494, Amazon, 2023.

Heat Engines: Thermodynamics, Cycles, & Performance Curves, ISBN-9798486886836, Amazon, 2021.

Heat Exchangers: Performance Prediction & Evaluation, ISBN-9781973589327, Amazon, 2017.

Heat Recovery Steam Generators: Thermal Design and Testing, ISBN-9781691029365, Amazon, 2019.

Heat Transfer: Heat Exchangers, Heat Recovery Steam Generators, & Cooling Towers, ISBN-9798487417831, Amazon, 2021.

Heat Transfer Examples: Practical Problems Solved, ISBN-9798390610763, Amazon, 2023.

The Kick-Start Murders: Visualize revenge, ISBN-9798759083375, Amazon, 2021.

Jamie2: Innocence is easily lost and cannot be restored, ISBN-9781520339375, Amazon, 2016-18.

Kyle Cooper Mysteries: Kick Start, Monte Carlo, and Waterfront Murders, ISBN-9798829365943, Amazon, 2022.

The Last Seraph: Sequel to Little Star, ISBN-9781726802253, Amazon, 2018.

Little Star: God doesn't do things the way we expect Him to. He's better than that! ISBN-9781520338903, Amazon, 2015-17.

Living Math: Seeing mathematics in every day life (and appreciating it more too), ISBN-9781520336992, Amazon, 2016.

Logic+Reason=>Truth: Thinking in the Age of Feeling, ISBN-9798333235022, Amazon, 2024.

Lost Cause: If only history could be changed..., ISBN-9781521173770, Amazon, 2017.

Mass Transfer: Diffusion & Convection, ISBN-9798702403106, Amazon, 2021.

Mill Town Destiny: The Hand of Providence brought them together to rescue the mill, the town, and each other, ISBN-9781520864679, Amazon, 2017.

Monte Carlo Murders: Who Killed Who and Why, ISBN-9798829341848, Amazon, 2022.

Monte Carlo Simulation: The Art of Random Process Characterization, ISBN-9781980577874, Amazon, 2018.

Nonlinear Equations: Numerical Methods for Solving, ISBN-9781717767318, Amazon, 2018.

Numerical Calculus: Differentiation and Integration, ISBN-9781980680901, Amazon, 2018.

Numerical Methods: Nonlinear Equations, Numerical Calculus, & Differential Equations, ISBN-9798486246845, Amazon, 2021.

Orthogonal Functions: The Many Uses of, ISBN-9781719876162, Amazon, 2018.

Overwhelming Evidence: A Pilgrimage, ISBN-9798515642211, Amazon, 2021.

Particle Tracking: Computational Strategies and Diverse Examples, ISBN-9781692512651, Amazon, 2019.

Plumes: Delineation & Transport, ISBN-9781702292771, Amazon, 2019.

Power Plant Performance Curves: for Testing and Dispatch, ISBN-9798640192698, Amazon, 2020.

Practical Linear Algebra: Principles & Software, ISBN-9798860910584, Amazon, 2023.

Props, Fans, & Pumps: Design & Performance, ISBN-9798645391195, Amazon, 2020.

Remediation: Contaminant Transport, Particle Tracking, & Plumes, ISBN-9798485651190, Amazon, 2021.

ROFL: Rolling on the Floor Laughing, ISBN-9781973300007, Amazon, 2017.

Seminole Rain: You don't choose destiny. It chooses you, ISBN-9798668502196, Amazon, 2020.

Septillionth: 1 in 10^{24}, ISBN-9798410762472, Amazon, 2022.

Software Development: Targeted Applications, ISBN-9798850653989, Amazon, 2023.

Software Recipes: Proven Tools, ISBN-9798815229556, Amazon, 2022.

Steam 2020: to 150 GPa and 6000 K, ISBN-9798634643830, Amazon, 2020.

Thermochemical Reactions: Numerical Solutions, ISBN-9781073417872, Amazon, 2019.

Thermodynamic and Transport Properties of Fluids, ISBN-9781092120845, Amazon, 2019.

Thermodynamic Cycles: Effective Modeling Strategies for Software Development, ISBN-9781070934372, Amazon, 2019.

Thermodynamics - Theory & Practice: The science of energy and power, ISBN-9781520339795, Amazon, 2016.

Version-Independent Programming: Code Development Guidelines for the Windows® Operating System, ISBN-9781520339146, Amazon, 2016.

The Waterfront Murders: As you sow, so shall you reap, ISBN-9798611314500, Amazon, 2020.

Weather Data: Where To Get It and How To Process It, ISBN-9798868037894, Amazon, 2023.